THE
SIMPLE
VEGAN
KITCHEN

NUTRITIONALLY BALANCED,
EASY AND DELICIOUS
PLANT-BASED MEALS FOR
DAILY WELLNESS

THE
SIMPLE
VEGAN
KITCHEN

LAUREN McNEILL, RD, MPH
CREATOR OF TASTING TO THRIVE

PAGE STREET
PUBLISHING CO.

PAGE STREET
PUBLISHING CO.

First published in 2023 by

Page Street Publishing Co.

27 Congress Street, Suite 1511

Salem, MA 01970

www.pagestreetpublishing.com

Distributed by Macmillan, sales in Canada by The Canadian Manda Group.

27 26 25 24 23   1 2 3 4 5

ISBN-13: 978-1-64567-724-6

ISBN-10: 1-64567-724-9

Library of Congress Control Number: 2022940202

Cover and book design by Laura Benton for Page Street Publishing Co.

Photography by Toni Zernik

Printed and bound in the United States of America

DEDICATION

TO AVERY, FOR BEING MY FOREVER
RECIPE TESTER

TO MOM, DAD, ANDREW AND JEFF,
FOR BELIEVING I COULD DO THIS
BEFORE I EVER DID

CONTENTS

INTRODUCTION

Welcome to *The Simple Vegan Kitchen*! Thank you so much for choosing this cookbook.

My passion for plant-based cooking and nutrition began when I decided to go vegetarian at 17. If you had told me back then that I'd be writing a plant-based cookbook, I probably wouldn't have believed you. I decided to go vegetarian for the animals, but I told myself that I'd never be vegan because I couldn't imagine giving up cheese. Fast forward through my journey of becoming a registered dietitian, getting my master's of public health in nutrition and starting my business, Tasting to Thrive, and I couldn't imagine it any other way.

When I first went vegetarian, I didn't know how to fuel myself properly, so I started experimenting with different ways of eating. You name it, I've tried it. Most "diets" that I tried focused heavily on restriction, highlighting what I *couldn't* eat rather than what I could eat, which just made me crave those foods more. I wanted to find a way of eating that made me feel good but that was sustainable and easy to follow during the busy seasons of life. I kept coming back to one truth: I wanted to eat in alignment with my values. I've always been a massive animal lover and knew that one of the best ways to support animal welfare was to stop contributing to the meat and dairy industry. I started transitioning from a vegetarian to a vegan diet when I was 21, and I slowly realized that I'd never felt better. Not only did I have more energy, deeper sleep and better overall wellness, but I also felt better mentally and emotionally. For the first time in a long time, I was eating in abundance and truly *enjoying* food.

I didn't really grow up cooking. I was lucky enough to have parents who cooked for my brothers and me every night, so cooking for myself was never really a necessity or something I was interested in. It wasn't until I transitioned to a plant-based eating style that I quickly realized that I would need to learn some cooking skills. I bought a few cookbooks and slowly began working my way through the recipes. I was shocked by how delicious and simple plant-based cooking could be and how *good* I felt after eating. I was feeling energized by my food and actually loving the process of creating delicious meals. Anyone who knows me now knows that I'm truly so passionate about creating food, from grocery shopping for delicious ingredients, to planning out what to eat, to cooking and serving food for friends and family. My mom even jokes that I don't care about gifts on holidays—it's all about the food for me.

Going vegetarian was a fairly quick and simple transition for me, but it took three years before I could say that I ate fully plant-based. I was wrapped up in so many different worries about what others would think of me, not wanting to be a burden and worrying that I would be missing out somehow. I also had a lot of questions during my transition to becoming fully vegan. Where was I supposed to get my protein? How would I make sure I was getting enough iron and calcium? And what would my meals look like without the traditional meat, veggie and starch plate breakdown? While I was confident that eating a plant-based diet could be super nutritious, I was confused about how to put these nutrition considerations into practice.

As I dove into the research and became more confident in my plant-based journey, I knew I had to find a way to inspire others to try more plant-based meals. To demystify plant-based nutrition myths and share that it is possible to get all of the nutrients you need on a plant-based diet, I started my Instagram page, @tastingtothrive_rd. My main motivation was to be a voice of evidence-based nutrition information in a sea of misinformation. I wanted to show people that eating plant-based didn't mean always eating salads and that we could eat the food we love while also taking care of ourselves. I could only have dreamt of it turning into what it has grown into today: a full-time business based on sharing recipes on social media and my blog, personalized nutrition coaching where I help clients one-on-one and my online programs.

My job as a dietitian is to translate the evidence-based knowledge we have about nutrition into attainable, actionable steps to make eating balanced, tasty and simple. But let me get one thing straight: This isn't a diet book. You won't see calorie counts, macronutrient breakdowns or any emphasis on eating as little as possible. You'll notice a pattern throughout this book. You'll notice that I like to focus on what we're adding to our everyday eating pattern, rather than what we're taking away. It's truly my philosophy that what we *are* eating is so much more important than what we *aren't* eating, and I hope I make that abundantly clear to you throughout. My motivation is always to help you feel your best, which comes down to eating for both satisfaction and for health. If you don't enjoy the food you're eating, chances are you won't feel very good, regardless of how "healthy" the food is.

This cookbook puts together the "what" and the "how" of plant-based eating. It's important to know what nutrients we need to be focusing on, like protein, iron and calcium, but it's equally important to understand how to put that into practice. Most of the recipes in this book are a great balance of protein, carbohydrates, fat and micronutrients to help you get there! Plus, they all taste amazing, meaning you'll fully enjoy the food that you're eating.

As a plant-based dietitian, this is the book I wish I'd had when I first started adopting a plant-based diet. Whether you're vegan, vegetarian or simply wanting to incorporate more plant-based foods into your everyday eating pattern, this book is for you. My goal is to share approachable, affordable, easy and delicious recipes that shed light on the fact that you don't need dairy, eggs or meat to make mouth-watering meals and snacks, and that you can eat balanced *and* enjoy your meals while doing so.

Whether you've been vegan for years or are just dipping your toes into trying more plant-based recipes, one thing remains true: We need to eat food that we enjoy, enough food for our bodies to thrive and in good variety so we feel our absolute best. I want you to know that wherever you are on your plant-based journey, you're welcome here.

L M'Nall

NOTE: Please remember that the information in this book is for educational purposes only and is not a replacement for personalized dietary advice from your team of health-care providers.

PLANT-BASED NUTRITION FOR BALANCED EVERYDAY EATING

First and foremost, let's define plant-based eating. There's no hard-and-fast definition for this term. Some believe that plant-based eating means eating vegan food in its most "natural" form, like vegetables, fruit, legumes, whole grains, nuts and seeds, and eating limited amounts of hyper-processed foods. Others believe plant-based means that someone eats a mostly vegan diet, while occasionally eating non-vegan food. For the purpose of this cookbook, the term "plant-based" means completely vegan recipes. Some recipes do include ingredients such as vegan cheese and vegan meat alternatives, but the majority use simple ingredients that can easily be found in most grocery stores.

Incorporating more plant-based foods often comes with a lot of questions, like "What should my meals look like?" "How do I make sure I'm getting enough nutrients?" and "Will I actually feel full?" These are questions that I hear all the time from my clients and through social media, and they're all valid. **The truth is that getting the nutrients you need on a plant-based diet can be really easy, but it does require a bit of understanding of how to create meals and snacks that are nourishing, well-balanced and delicious.**

THE MACRONUTRIENTS

In short, macronutrients are the nutrients we need a lot of. Protein, carbohydrates and fat are macro-nutrients, and despite what you might hear about the latest fad diet, getting all three of them daily, in adequate quantities, is important for our bodies to function properly.

PROTEIN

If I had a dime for every time someone asked me how to get enough protein on a plant-based diet, I'd be a millionaire. But, to be honest, I actually encourage the question! So many of us grew up thinking that we could only get protein from meat and dairy, but in reality, that's just not the case.

Many plant foods are rich in protein, such as beans, lentils, other legumes, tofu, tempeh, edamame, soy milk, soy curls, textured vegetable protein, seitan and vegan meat alternatives. You'll notice that most of the recipes in this cookbook use these protein-rich foods to help you easily meet your protein needs in simple, delicious ways.

So how much protein do we actually need? **Research shows that most people need about 0.9 to 1.3 grams of protein per kilogram of their body weight, or about half of their weight in pounds in grams of protein** (Tome 2012; WHO 2007). For example, if someone weighs 150 pounds, they would need approximately 75 grams of protein per day.

This amount is easily obtained by aiming to make about a quarter of our meals plant-based, protein-rich foods. This could look like adding ½ cup (135 g) of white beans into a pasta recipe, stirring a can of lentils into a soup or roasting some chick-peas to add to a salad.

Different protein-rich foods contain different amino acids, which are the building blocks of protein. Because of this, it's important to include a variety of protein-rich foods into your daily eating pattern. I recommend switching up your sources of protein between beans, lentils, soy products and different vegan meat alternatives to achieve this variety.

Getting enough protein doesn't have to be complicated, and as long as you're eating enough food for your body and including protein-rich foods at most meals, getting enough protein likely won't be an issue.

While true protein deficiency is very uncommon, signs that you may not be getting enough include feeling especially hungry between meals, mood swings, loss in muscle mass despite working out regularly and weakening of hair, skin and nails.

CARBOHYDRATES

Our bodies run on carbohydrates. They're the primary and preferred source of fuel, but somehow carbohydrates have still fallen prey to being demonized by diet culture (Goyal and Raichle, 2018). Let me make one thing clear: There is absolutely no reason to fear carbohydrates. In fact, much of the research that we have on the healthiest populations on the planet, the Blue Zones, show that one thing is clear—they eat plenty of whole grains and fiber-rich carbohydrates (Aune, Dagfinn et al. 2016).

But what really *is* fiber? Most of us know that fiber helps us to have healthy bowel movements (hello, prunes), but it does so much more than that. **Fiber helps us to feel fuller for longer, to regulate our blood sugar, feed our beneficial gut bacteria and, yes, to have healthy, well-formed bowel movements.**

Studies show that only 5 percent of North Americans meet their daily fiber requirements (Quagliani and Felt-Gunderson 2017). In general, women should aim for 25 grams per day, whereas men should aim for 38 grams per day, but this is really a ballpark estimate based on your calorie intake (Quagliani and Felt-Gunderson 2017). Because I don't recommend counting calories, my guideline is to aim for at least three to four servings of fiber-rich foods per day.

Great sources of fiber-rich carbohydrates include, but aren't limited to, brown rice, whole wheat bread, whole wheat pasta, beans, lentils, potatoes and fruit.

As you're probably noticing, I'm emphasizing whole grains. Whole grains mean that they have the whole grain intact, rather than removing parts of the grain, such as in white bread, white rice and white pasta. With that being said, not all grains you eat need to be whole grains. It's important to acknowledge that many foods that are an important part of cultural dishes or are simply preferred, such as white rice, rice noodles and white breads, are not whole grains, and that's completely okay. **I recommend aiming to choose whole grains at least 50 percent of the time to help meet fiber requirements, while fully acknowledging that you can also get fiber from other foods like beans, legumes and fruit.**

Signs that you may need to up your carbohydrate intake include low energy, intense cravings for carbohydrate-rich foods, constipation or diarrhea and headaches.

FAT

Another macronutrient that doesn't get enough credit is fat. **Fat is so important for absorbing vitamins A, D, E and K. It also helps our body with hormonal regulation and to feel satisfied from our food** (Lepretti, Marilena et al. 2018). From a cooking perspective, fat helps to carry flavor, like spices and salt, and improves the mouthfeel of food.

Diet culture either demonizes or idolizes fat. In the '80s and '90s, the low-fat diet was all the rage, whereas we recently saw an upswing in the ketogenic diet (which was originally developed for children with epilepsy), where large amounts of fat are encouraged. So how much fat should we really be eating? As with most things in nutrition, the answer lies somewhere in the middle of these two diet trends.

As a general guideline, about 20 to 25 percent of our calories should come from fat, with only 5 to 6 percent being from saturated fat. To meet these requirements, I recommend adding a source of fat to most meals and snacks.

Not all fat is created equal. Mono- and polyunsaturated fats have health-promoting effects, like helping to prevent heart disease and reducing LDL ("bad") cholesterol, whereas saturated fat and trans fats should be limited or avoided altogether, respectively, as they can increase the risk of developing heart disease (Liu et al. 2017). Saturated fat is harder to come by on a plant-based diet, with the predominant sources being coconut oil and palm oil. However, with the uptick of more plant-based meat alternatives and cheeses, some of which use coconut or palm oil in their ingredients, it is worth being aware of the amount of saturated fat in these products. This doesn't mean you can never eat your favorite vegan meats and cheeses (I even include a few recipes with them in this book!), but instead I encourage you to eat these a few times per week if you love them, rather than every day.

One type of fat that we should all be aiming to include regularly is omega-3. Getting an adequate amount of omega-3 is vital for the anti-inflammatory response in our body and helps to maintain good brain, heart and eye health.

When most of us think omega-3, the first thing that comes to mind is fish. But did you know that fish eat algae, and that's where they get *their* omega-3? Instead of eating fish, we can get omega-3 from an algae-based omega-3 supplement or even from specific nuts and seeds like flax, chia, hemp and walnuts. I recommend aiming to eat 2 to 3 tablespoons of chia, flax or hemp seeds per day, or about ¼ cup of walnuts, to meet omega-3 needs. Flax seeds should be ground, as they can be tough for our bodies to fully break down on their own.

Other foods that are great sources of fat are avocados, olives, nuts, seeds, nut and seed butters and certain oils, like olive and avocado. I recommend aiming to incorporate a source of fat with most meals to keep you feeling full and satisfied and to help absorb important nutrients. Symptoms of not eating enough fat can include poor absorption of vitamins A, D, E and K, a weakened immune system and dry skin and hair.

THE MICRONUTRIENTS

Just like macronutrients are the nutrients that you need a lot of, micronutrients are the ones you need a *little* bit of. But just because you only need a little bit of them doesn't mean they aren't important!

While it's totally possible to get the nutrients you need on a plant-based diet, there are some that we need to be more aware of than others. This isn't an exhaustive list of the most important nutrients, but rather a guide for the ones that may need a little more attention than others and how to make sure you're getting enough of them.

For specific supplement recommendations, I always recommend getting regular blood work done and working with a registered dietitian, ideally one who specializes in plant-based nutrition, to assess what is right for you.

VITAMIN B12

Vitamin B12 is important for memory and cognition, forming red blood cells and maintaining good energy levels (Reynolds, 2006). It's a nutrient formed by bacteria that used to be readily available in the soil, but since our soils are so depleted, we now need to rely on food sources or supplements.

While there are some fortified plant-based foods that contain vitamin B12, such as some plant-based milks, nutritional yeast and vegan meat alternatives, **I suggest that most people who follow a plant-based diet take a vitamin B12 supplement.** This is because the types of food that we eat on a daily basis, as well as the amount of food, can vary so much.

IRON

The next question after "How do I get enough protein?" is always "Can I get enough iron on a plant-based diet?" **But did you know that iron deficiency anemia is just as common in those who eat an omnivorous diet as in those who eat a well-planned plant-based diet (Saunders et al. 2013)?**

The key term here is "well-planned." While this might sound intimidating, it really just means **making a conscious effort to incorporate iron-rich foods regularly, at least two to three servings per day. Some plant-based foods that are high in iron include black beans, lentils, tofu, tempeh, edamame, dark, leafy greens like kale, bok choy and broccoli, sprouted bread, oats and dried fruit.**

There are also some strategies we can use to help our bodies absorb iron more effectively. Try pairing iron-rich foods with foods that contain vitamin C to help increase absorption four- to sixfold (Lane and Richardson 2014). Foods that are high in vitamin C include bell peppers, broccoli, citrus fruit, strawberries, cantaloupe and kale. You can also try cooking your meals with cast-iron cookware, as it can add some iron to the food. It's also a good idea to avoid drinking coffee or tea with iron-rich foods, as they can decrease iron absorption. Lastly, if you take a calcium supplement, try to avoid taking it with food, as supplemental calcium can inhibit the absorption of iron (IOM 1998; Millward 2007).

CALCIUM

You've probably heard that we need to drink milk to have healthy bones and teeth, but is that true?

Despite what people may think, cow's milk *isn't* the only source of calcium. **In fact, most store-bought plant-based milks are fortified with the same amount of calcium and vitamin D as cow's milk, meaning they can be a one-for-one milk replacement.** I recommend choosing soy or pea milk, which boast 7 to 8 grams of protein per cup, whereas other plant-based milks like almond, soy and cashew usually have between 1 and 4 grams per cup. Most people who follow a plant-based diet should aim to include 1 cup (240 ml) of calcium-fortified plant-based milk per day to easily get about one-third of their daily calcium needs.

Other great plant-based sources of calcium include almonds, almond butter, tahini, black strap molasses, dark leafy greens like kale, bok choy and broccoli, white beans, oranges and figs.

We can also get a significant amount of calcium from calcium-set tofu, tempeh and edamame. Aim for at least 3 cups of these calcium-rich foods per day to help meet your calcium needs.

While some studies have shown that eating a vegan or vegetarian diet may increase the risk of bone fractures, these studies were done on populations that weren't getting adequate amounts of calcium or protein (Menzel et al. 2021). It's also important to note that while calcium absolutely plays an important role in bone health, it isn't the *only* factor. Other factors, both controllable and uncontrollable, play a huge role in bone health, such as genetics, family history, getting enough vitamin D, protein, calcium and magnesium, engaging in weight-bearing physical activity and reducing alcohol consumption.

IODINE

Iodine is an often-overlooked nutrient, but one that's so important to make sure you're getting enough of, whether you follow a plant-based diet or not.

In North America, it became apparent that many people weren't getting enough iodine naturally from food, which is why many governments decided to iodize salt. Now, with the popularity of sea salt and pink Himalayan salt, both of which aren't typically iodized, some people may not be getting enough iodine in their diet.

Iodine is important for thyroid health and for ensuring proper fetal development in pregnancy. **I recommend using iodized salt for your cooking.** It's an easy way to ensure you're getting enough iodine in your daily eating pattern, as about half a teaspoon meets most adults' daily needs. Unfortunately, most pink Himalayan and sea salts aren't fortified with iodine. If you're adamant about using these, you may need to take an iodine supplement. While seaweed can be a source of iodine, the amount varies between types and brands of seaweed, so I wouldn't recommend relying on this as a source of iodine unless amounts are clearly stated on the label (Zimmermann 2009).

SELENIUM

Selenium is an antioxidant that helps to maintain proper immune function and fertility and to protect against certain diseases (Cardoso et al. 2017). Plant-based sources of selenium include Brazil nuts, and to a lesser extent, soy foods, peanuts and grains. One large Brazil nut per day is all you need to meet your selenium requirements, so I recommend adding this in! While we should be meeting our selenium needs, more isn't always better, so I wouldn't recommend eating more than 3 to 5 Brazil nuts per day. This is the perfect example of "more isn't always better," as exceeding daily selenium requirements has detrimental effects on the body, too.

ZINC

Zinc is a mineral that's important for immune function, sexual health and wound healing (Maret, Wolfgang and Sandstead 2006). While zinc can be found in smaller quantities in many plant-based foods, it's a nutrient that's often overlooked, and we need to ensure we're eating enough to meet our needs. Men should aim for 11 mg per day, and women should aim for 8 mg per day. **It can be found in legumes, nuts, seeds, whole grains and tofu.**

VITAMIN D

Vitamin D, the sunshine vitamin, is one of the nutrients that you're most likely to be deficient in if you live somewhere that experiences a true winter, with about three-quarters of the North American population being deficient (Ginde, Adit, Liu and Camargo 2009; Schwalfenberg, Genuis and Hiltz 2010). Most of us know that our bodies can make vitamin D from sun exposure, but if you live somewhere where sunshine is a limited resource throughout the winter, it's important to make sure you're getting enough through food or supplements. Some plant-based foods are fortified with vitamin D, such as plant-based milks, but regardless of whether you follow a plant-based diet or not, most people in North America can benefit from including a vitamin D supplement regularly.

SOY

It would be impossible for me to write a plant-based cookbook and not address the rumors surrounding soy. Soy has gotten an undeserved bad rap over the years for completely unfounded reasons.

Soybeans contain phytoestrogens, *plant estrogens*, called isoflavones. These isoflavones can bind to estrogen receptor sites; **however, plant estrogens are not the same as human estrogen and have significantly weaker activity.** Human studies show that consuming soy in typical amounts of two to three servings per day does not have an effect on testosterone levels (Hamilton et al. 2010). Isoflavones can act on reproductive cells, such as breast and uterus tissue, as very weak antiestrogens and on bone with a weak estrogen-like effect, both of which are *good things* for our health (Oseni, Patel, Pyle and Jordan 2008; Chen and Anderson 2002).

Research shows that lifetime soy consumption may actually be *protective* against breast cancer, improve breast cancer prognosis and reduce the risk of breast cancer recurrence or death. Soy consumption has also been linked with a decreased risk of prostate cancer and prostate cancer cell growth (Oseni, Patel, Pyle and Jordan 2008; van Die, Bone, Williams and Pirotta 2014; Ahmad et al. 2010; Yan and Spitznagel 2009). Soy consumption has also been shown to be beneficial for reducing the risk of cardiovascular disease. The evidence of these beneficial effects is strongest at two to three servings per day of traditional soy foods, like soy milk, tofu, tempeh and edamame.

Soy consumption may affect the thyroid gland in the very small number of people who have hypothyroidism or who are deficient in iodine. For those individuals, it makes sense to consult your healthcare team to limit soy consumption or adjust necessary medication to allow for soy consumption (Messina 2010; Marini et al. 2012; Messina, Watanabe and Setchell 2009).

The take-home message? Soy is just a type of bean, and its effects can be primarily neutral or positive for our health.

THE BALANCED PLATE APPROACH

Now that we've covered the "what" in terms of eating, let's talk about the "how." It's all well and good to understand the types of food, vitamins and minerals we need and to make sure we're getting enough of them but it's more important to actually be able to incorporate these foods easily into our regular eating pattern.

To make this easier, I like to use the Balanced Plate approach, which aims to create most meals around the inclusion of veggies and/or fruit, plant-based protein, whole grains or starchy veggies and fat. **Aim for about half a plate of vegetables or fruit, a quarter plate of plant-based protein, a quarter plate of whole grains or starchy veggies and a source of fat with each meal.** The exact portion sizes will vary based on each individual's needs, but this approach is a good place to start. If you're active, increasing the portion of carbohydrates and protein and decreasing the amount of vegetables and fruit can be helpful. Following these guidelines will not only ensure that you're getting a good balance of protein, carbohydrates and fat, but it will also aid you in getting a good variety of vitamins, minerals and fiber to help you feel more nourished and energized throughout the day.

This method ensures that you're still eating the foods you love, while keeping gentle nutrition in mind, too. **Instead of focusing on *taking away* certain aspects of your plate, focus on what you can add to it.** For example, can you add lentils to rice or pasta for some plant-based protein? Add a handful of spinach to the sauce for some veggies? And maybe add a sprinkle of hemp seeds for some omega-3-rich fats? Small adjustments make a big difference!

When it comes to snacks, aim to get at least two of these four food groups in: protein, carbs, fiber and fat. This could look like pairing an apple (carbs and fiber) with peanut butter (fat), some Sweet & Spicy Edamame from page 140 (protein and fat) with sliced veggies (fiber) or a few Lemon-Coconut Energy Balls from page 147 (fat and fiber!).

You'll notice that a lot of plant-based meals don't have perfectly portioned sections of protein, carbohydrates, veggies and fat like your typical meat, potato and veggie meal. That's okay! The point is to notice whether you have these components at *most* (not necessarily all!) meals. This is a *guideline*, not something prescriptive that needs to be followed exactly. There will absolutely be meals where following this methodology isn't possible, or isn't even wanted. That's okay—what you eat most of the time is so much more important than what you eat some of the time.

I've taken the guesswork out of it by creating most of the recipes in this cookbook to follow these guidelines and help with the *how* of incorporating more plant-based foods and ensuring you're getting the nutrients you need. By including the breakfast, lunch, dinner and snack recipes outlined in this book in your regular eating pattern, you should meet your nutrient needs easily. If you have a lunch that's lower in veggies, try choosing a dinner that has more veggies! The same goes for plant-based protein, fiber and fat. This way you can aim to have a good balance throughout the day, rather than stressing over each specific meal.

If you need additional guidance, try using the meal plan on page 151 in the back of the book!

A NOTE ON INTUITIVE EATING

You might think that it's my job as a dietitian to tell you what to eat, but in reality, that's not how I like to do things. **I believe in intuitive eating, which means listening to what your body is craving and honoring those cravings while finding opportunities for gentle nutrition**. You'll also notice that throughout this book, I don't refer to any food as "good," "bad," "healthy" or "unhealthy." It's all just food. Sometimes we eat for enjoyment, sometimes we eat for fuel and a lot of the time it's a little bit of both.

Many of my clients say they feel out of control around certain foods, like they can't stop at one bowl of chips, a few pieces of chocolate or just one cookie. They feel like food is controlling them, rather than feeling in control around food. Most people are shocked when I tell them that if they're feeling uncontrollable around certain foods, chances are they actually aren't eating *enough* of them.

How can that be the case? Well, our body is much smarter than we are. When we try to restrict foods, we start to crave them more. Have you ever sworn off chocolate, only to find yourself elbow deep in chocolate bars a few days later? You're not alone, and the problem isn't you. The problem is diet culture telling us that we have to restrict these types of foods, that balance isn't good enough and that you're somehow "bad" for wanting them.

The solution? Introduce these foods more often while also ensuring you're eating enough food in general, and have a good balance of protein, carbohydrates, fat and fiber.

What does this look like in practice? To be honest, it looks a little bit different every day based on how hungry you are, your energy levels, what you're craving and what food you have available to you. In some cases, it might mean eating pasta because it's what your body is craving but choosing to add some white beans, like in my One-Pan Mushroom Gnocchi (page 50), because you know they'll be a great source of protein and fiber to help you feel full for longer. On other days, it might mean choosing the salad with quinoa and tofu because your body needs more veggies or choosing the pizza and not concerning yourself over the veggies because you know there are other eating opportunities throughout the day. **Remember that what we eat most of the time is so much more important than what we eat some of the time.**

FEELING SATISFIED BY YOUR FOOD

If you're worried about feeling satisfied by your food on a plant-based diet, you're not alone. That's one of the most common concerns I get from clients and through social media, and I'm here to help! There are so many factors that play into feeling satisfied from our food, but here are three of the main components.

EATING ENOUGH

Most plant-based foods are less energy dense than animal-based foods. This means we need to eat *more* in order to feel full. I consider this to be a huge benefit of plant-based eating!

If you're noticing that you don't feel completely satisfied after eating, try increasing the portion sizes of your meals or including an additional snack throughout the day.

ENSURING A GOOD BALANCE OF FOOD

Getting a good balance of protein, carbohydrates, fat and fiber helps to keep us feeling more satisfied from our food and our blood sugar balanced, so we can avoid those peaks and valleys from eating.

Take some time to assess whether you're getting a good balance of these foods at most meals. If you usually eat plain oatmeal for breakfast, can you add a spoonful of peanut butter to make it more filling? Or cook it in soy milk rather than water for some extra protein? Maybe you can add a handful of berries to add some color, volume and fiber. Experiment and see what works for you!

Something we haven't touched on, but that I'd argue is the *most* important part of eating, is enjoying your food. If you don't like what you're eating, chances are you're never going to feel satisfied from it.

When it comes to eating, it's important to listen to both our inner and outer knowledge. Inner knowledge accepts the food that you *know* you're craving and likely won't feel satisfied without eating, which can change on a daily basis. For example, pasta. Outer knowledge is the gentle nutrition piece that tells you that while pasta is a great source of carbohydrates, it's not as good of a source of protein, fat or veggies. Remember, this is why we focus on *adding* to our plate rather than taking away. Another way to think of that concept is that we honor our *inner* knowledge by making the pasta we're craving for dinner, yet we also honor our *outer* knowledge by understanding that we'll feel more satisfied and fuller for longer if we add protein, fiber and fat to that pasta.

This is a brief, simplified explanation for something that can be complicated, nuanced and downright hard to do with diet culture constantly telling us what we *should* eat. We've placed such heavy restrictions on our eating that we think if we allow ourselves to have full reign of eating whatever we want, we'll automatically stuff our faces with donuts, chips and chocolate all day long. But have you ever come back from a vacation with lots of fun, indulgent food and craved a salad? That's a real-life example of intuitive eating working in real time. **When we actually allow ourselves to eat the food that diet culture tells us we need to avoid at all costs, it loses power over us and becomes less enticing.**

There are other ways we can ensure we enjoy our food, too:

Salt: While we want to be cognizant of the amount of salt that we add to our food, if we're cooking from home most often with whole, plant-based foods, we don't need to worry too much, as most excessive salt is found in packaged, hyper-processed foods. Adding additional salt to a recipe elevates the flavor and makes it more palatable.

Seasoning: Adding proper seasoning to food is so important to make it taste good! For example, if you hate tofu, chances are you aren't seasoning it properly. Using sauces, spices, garlic, onion, salt and pepper goes such a long way in cooking.

Acid: Sometimes it just tastes like there's something *missing* in a dish, and a lot of the time this can be fixed by adding something acidic, like a squeeze of lemon or lime, a dash of apple cider vinegar or some white wine.

Texture: Adding crunch, creaminess or chewiness to a dish can elevate it to the next level. This can often be done by adding toppings to a soup, like croutons or crispy chickpeas, putting some nuts or seeds to a salad or having crisp, crunchy lettuce on a sandwich. If you're craving something creamy, introduce healthy fats to your plate or bowl with some avocado. Want a flavorful chew? Add some egg-free noodles to broths and slurp to your heart's delight.

Now that we understand the basics of how to create balanced meals and snacks, let's get cooking!

HEARTY
MAINS

I'm a firm believer that our meals should be just as delicious as they are satisfying and nutritious. Bonus points if they're super easy and cost-effective, too! When I first became plant-based, I relied on one-pot and one-pan meals a ton, both for their convenience and easy cleanup. Nowadays, I like to switch it up a little bit more, but I still stand behind the philosophy of having four or five recipes that you love and know how to make easily for those days when you just don't know what to cook. These hearty mains are quick, easy, delicious and should help you do just that.

As a busy dietitian and entrepreneur, I totally understand the struggle of wanting something nourishing and satisfying that doesn't take forever to make. For those days, I rely on meals like my Spicy Creamy Fusilli Pasta (page 39), 15-Minute Sun-dried Tomatoes & White Beans (page 35) or Lemon-Dill Potato Sheet Pan Meal (page 27). On days that I have a little bit more time and energy, I love to make a big pot of my Smoky Black Bean Chili (page 49) to have throughout the week or my Herby Lentil "Meatballs" & Garlic Bread (page 42). If you're able to, I highly recommend making more than you need and having leftovers for lunch or dinner the next day.

I hope that some of these recipes get added to your weekly rotation and that you love them as much as I do!

WARMING VEGETABLE & CHICKPEA CURRY

Curries are perfect for those nights when you don't really know what to cook, have a bunch of veggies in your fridge to use up and want something hearty and nourishing. This Warming Vegetable & Chickpea Curry uses carrots, sweet potatoes and broccoli, but feel free to switch up the veggies based on what you have on hand. The curry flavor pairs perfectly with fresh ginger and garlic. It takes about 30 minutes to throw together and can be served on its own or with rice to make it more filling.

SERVES 5

PREP: 10 MINUTES
COOK: 30 MINUTES
TOTAL: 40 MINUTES

1. In a large pot over medium heat, heat the olive oil. Add the onion and sauté it until it's translucent, about 3 to 4 minutes.

2. Add the garlic, ginger, carrots, broccoli, sweet potato, bell pepper, curry powder and salt. Sauté them for another 2 to 3 minutes.

3. Add the canned tomatoes (with the juices), coconut milk and chickpeas. Place the lid on the pot, and increase the heat to high to bring the curry to a low boil, which takes about 5 minutes.

4. Once the curry is at a low boil, reduce the heat to low-medium, and let it simmer for 20 to 25 minutes with the lid on, until the sweet potatoes and carrots are tender.

5. Serve it with rice, lime juice and cilantro, if desired.

RECIPE NOTES: If you like your curry thicker, feel free to cook it with the lid off.

The flavor of your curry will partially depend on the type of curry powder you choose. I used a mild curry powder in this recipe.

1 tbsp (15 ml) olive oil

1 yellow onion, diced

4 cloves garlic, minced

1½ tbsp (8 g) minced fresh ginger

1½ cups (192 g) diced carrots

1 cup (91 g) broccoli florets

1 large sweet potato, diced

1 red bell pepper, diced

2½ tbsp (24 g) curry powder

1 tsp salt

1 (28-oz [794-ml]) can diced tomatoes

1 (14-oz [400-ml]) can coconut milk

1 (19-oz [540-g]) can chickpeas, drained and rinsed

Cooked rice, for serving, optional

Fresh lime juice, for serving, optional

Chopped cilantro, for serving, optional

CREAMY GARLIC-LEMON PASTA

This is a family-friendly meal that's super decadent and hearty while still being totally plant-based. We use sunflower seeds as a replacement for heavy cream, and butter, cherry tomatoes and lemon to brighten up the dish. If you want an extra boost of plant-based protein in this pasta, feel free to add some white beans when you're mixing the pasta and sauce together. I promise that this pasta will convince even the most stubborn plant-based-hesitant people that pasta without butter or cream can still taste amazing.

4 cloves garlic, minced

2 tbsp (30 ml) olive oil, divided

1 cup (134 g) raw, hulled, unsalted sunflower seeds

4 tbsp (60 ml) lemon juice, about 1 lemon

¼ cup (44 g) nutritional yeast

¾ cup (180 ml) plant-based milk, plus more as needed (I used unsweetened oat milk)

¾ tsp salt, plus 1 tsp for salting the pasta water

¼ tsp pepper

16 oz (450 g) fettuccine

2 cups (300 g) cherry tomatoes

1. In a large pan over low-medium heat, sauté the garlic in 1 tablespoon (15 ml) of olive oil until the garlic is lightly golden brown, being careful not to burn it, about 2 minutes.

2. Transfer the garlic to a high-speed blender with the sunflower seeds, lemon juice, nutritional yeast, plant-based milk, salt and pepper. Blend them until the mixture is completely smooth, adding additional plant-based milk 1 tablespoon (15 ml) at a time, if needed.

3. Meanwhile, cook the fettuccine per package instructions in well-salted water. Reserve ½ cup (120 ml) of the pasta water, then drain the pasta.

4. In the same pan you sautéed the garlic in, sauté the cherry tomatoes in the remaining 1 tablespoon (15 ml) of olive oil over medium heat and cover. Let the tomatoes sit for 3 to 4 minutes to blister, then stir them every 2 to 3 minutes until they burst. You can use the back of a spoon to burst them if necessary. Once the tomatoes have burst, remove them from the heat and place them in a bowl.

5. Pour the pasta sauce into the pan and heat it gently over low-medium heat. Add the cooked pasta to the sauce and mix it until it's combined, adding a splash of pasta water to further moisten the pasta, if needed. Add the cherry tomatoes to the pasta, mix to combine, serve and enjoy.

6. Refrigerate leftovers in an airtight container for up to 4 days.

RECIPE NOTE: When reheating leftovers, add a splash of plant-based milk to moisten the pasta.

LEMON-DILL POTATO SHEET PAN MEAL

Sheet pan meals are a delicious way to get a meal on the table quickly with minimal effort, and this Lemon-Dill Potato Sheet Pan Meal is no exception. It has a great balance of plant-based protein from the chickpeas, carbohydrates and fiber from the potatoes, veggies from the Brussels sprouts and healthy fats from the tahini lemon sauce. This is a great recipe to meal prep since it can be made all on one pan and the leftovers store well.

1. Preheat the oven to 450°F (232°C). Line two baking sheets with parchment paper.

2. For the sheet pan portion of the meal, place the baby potatoes, chickpeas and Brussels sprouts in a large bowl. Add the olive oil, garlic, fresh dill, lemon juice, salt and pepper, and mix them until they're well combined.

3. Add the mixture to the sheet pans, making sure to space the potatoes evenly so that the ingredients roast rather than steam. Roast them for 35 to 40 minutes, flipping them halfway through, until the potatoes are golden brown and fork tender.

4. Meanwhile, make the sauce. Whisk together the tahini, garlic powder, lemon juice, nutritional yeast, maple syrup, water, dill and salt for the tahini lemon sauce. You could also use a blender for this step.

5. Once the sheet pan ingredients have cooked, serve them in a bowl and drizzle the tahini lemon sauce on top.

6. Refrigerate the sheet pan ingredients and lemon tahini sauce separately in airtight containers for up to 5 days.

RECIPE NOTES: The smaller you cut the potatoes and Brussels sprouts, the faster they'll cook. Avoid overcrowding the sheet pan, since doing so will cause the veggies and chickpeas to steam rather than roast. This goes for roasting anything!

GOOD SOURCE OF PROTEIN, ONE-POT MEAL

SERVES 4

PREP: 15 MINUTES
COOK: 35–40 MINUTES
TOTAL: 50–55 MINUTES

FOR THE SHEET PAN
1½ lb (680 g) baby potatoes, halved

1 (19-oz [540-g]) can chickpeas, drained and rinsed

3½ cups (308 g) Brussels sprouts, quartered

2 tbsp (30 ml) olive oil

5 cloves garlic, minced

3 tbsp (1½ g) fresh dill, chopped

2 tbsp (30 ml) lemon juice, about ½ lemon

1 tsp salt, or to taste

¼ tsp pepper

FOR THE SAUCE
¼ cup (60 g) tahini

½ tsp garlic powder

2 tbsp (30 ml) lemon juice, about ½ lemon

1 tbsp (11 g) nutritional yeast

1½ tsp (7 ml) maple syrup

2 tbsp (30 ml) water, plus more as needed

1 tsp fresh dill, chopped

½ tsp salt

MISO-GINGER TOFU STIR-FRY

Stir-fries are one of my go-to recipes when I know I want something warm and nourishing but don't feel like spending forever cooking. Umami is something that can often be lacking in plant-based cooking, but rest assured, the miso in this stir-fry is packed with it! I've made this Miso-Ginger Tofu Stir-Fry with bell pepper, onion, broccoli and green beans, but feel free to sub out the vegetables based on your own personal preference and what you have on hand. Using frozen veggies instead of fresh for this recipe means it comes together even quicker! This stir-fry tastes amazing on its own, but it can also be served with rice or noodles for a more well-rounded, filling meal.

FOR THE MARINADE

2 tbsp (34 g) white miso paste

2 tbsp (10 g) minced fresh ginger

2 tbsp (30 ml) soy sauce

2 tbsp (30 ml) rice vinegar

2 tbsp (30 ml) sesame oil

2 cloves garlic, minced

FOR THE STIR-FRY

1 (12-oz [350-g]) block extra firm tofu, cut into 1-inch (2.5-cm) cubes

1 tbsp (15 ml) olive oil

1 red bell pepper, diced

¼ red onion, sliced

2 cups (182 g) broccoli florets

8 oz (225 g) green beans, halved, with the ends removed

1. In a large bowl, whisk together the miso paste, ginger, soy sauce, rice vinegar, sesame oil and garlic for the marinade.

2. Add the cubed tofu and mix it well until the tofu is coated in the marinade. Cover the bowl with plastic wrap and place it in the fridge to marinate for at least 30 minutes.

3. To begin the stir-fry, in a large pan over medium heat, sauté the bell pepper, red onion, broccoli and green beans in the olive oil for 5 to 7 minutes, or until they're tender.

4. Once the tofu has marinated, add the entire contents of the bowl, including the marinade, to the pan with the vegetables. Cook it for 10 to 15 minutes, sautéing and flipping the tofu every 2 to 3 minutes until it's lightly golden brown on all sides.

5. Refrigerate any leftovers in an airtight container for 3 to 4 days.

RECIPE NOTES: The smaller you cut the tofu, the more flavor it'll soak up from the marinade.

I recommend letting the tofu marinate in the miso ginger sauce for 30 minutes or longer for optimal flavor, but if you don't have enough time, you can also just pour the marinade ingredients into the pan and sauté them together, with the understanding that it may not be quite as flavorful.

SUN-DRIED TOMATO & BRUSSELS SPROUTS PASTA

GOOD SOURCE
OF PROTEIN,
ONE-POT MEAL

SERVES 5

PREP: 10 MINUTES
COOK: 20-25 MINUTES
TOTAL: 30-35 MINUTES

This is my mom's favorite pasta, and for good reason. It has the same comforting feel as regular pasta while still being a great source of fiber, protein and veggies. It stores beautifully as leftovers, making it a great meal to create at the beginning of a busy week when you know you won't have much time to get dinner on the table. This pasta recipe relies on the flavor from the sun-dried tomatoes, nutritional yeast and lemon rather than a sauce, making it taste much lighter. I encourage you to play around with the portions of these ingredients to meet your taste preferences!

1. In a large pan over medium heat, sauté the Brussels sprouts in the olive oil for 7 to 10 minutes until they're lightly charred, flipping only occasionally.

2. Add the mushrooms and garlic, and sauté them for another 5 minutes, or until the liquid has released and evaporated from the mushrooms. Meanwhile, cook the pasta in well-salted pasta water, as per the package instructions. Once the pasta has finished cooking, reserve 1 cup (240 ml) of pasta water, then drain the pasta. You may not need all of the reserved pasta water.

3. Add the sun-dried tomatoes and 1 tablespoon (15 ml) of the oil from the jar to the pan, plus the salt and pepper. Sauté them to combine. Pour the wine into the pan to deglaze.

4. Add the pasta to the pan with the veggies, along with ¼ cup (60 ml) of the reserved pasta water. Add the white beans, lemon juice, nutritional yeast, another drizzle of oil from the sun-dried tomatoes and chili flakes, if using.

5. Stir to combine everything. Feel free to add more pasta water if the pasta is too dry. You can also add more nutritional yeast for a cheesier flavor, more salt or pepper or more lemon juice for a bright tanginess.

6. Refrigerate any leftovers in an airtight container for up to 5 days.

RECIPE NOTE: If you stir the Brussels sprouts too often they won't get that beautiful brown char and won't be as flavorful.

4½ cups (396 g) Brussels sprouts, quartered

1 tbsp (15 ml) olive oil

8 oz (227 g) cremini mushrooms, sliced

4 cloves garlic, minced

16 oz (450 g) fusilli pasta

½ cup (27 g) oil-packed sun-dried tomatoes, sliced (reserve the remaining oil in the jar)

1 tsp salt, plus more as needed

¼ tsp pepper, plus more as needed

½ cup (120 ml) white wine or no-salt-added vegetable stock

1 (19-oz [540-g]) can white beans, drained and rinsed

4 tbsp (60 ml) lemon juice, about 1 lemon, plus more as needed

¼ cup (44 g) nutritional yeast, plus more if desired

¼ tsp chili flakes, optional

APPLE-DILL CHICKPEA MASH

SERVES 4

PREP: 15 MINUTES
TOTAL: 15 MINUTES

This Apple-Dill Chickpea Mash is a lunchtime staple in my house for a reason: It's quick, easy and packed with flavor! Plus, it's a great way to add an extra serving of beans into your day and is totally kid-approved. If you struggle with finding a way to eat beans that you enjoy, this recipe is the perfect introduction! I love serving this chickpea mash on toast, in a wrap or in a salad.

1 (19-oz [540-g]) can chickpeas, drained and rinsed

1 cup (101 g) diced celery, about 2 stalks

1 red bell pepper, diced

1 apple, chopped (I used Gala)

¼ red onion, diced

3 tbsp (45 ml) vegan mayonnaise

1 tbsp (15 ml) Dijon mustard

2 tbsp (1 g) fresh dill, chopped

2 tbsp (30 ml) freshly squeezed lemon juice

½ tsp garlic powder

¼ tsp salt, or to taste

¼ tsp pepper, or to taste

FOR SERVING

For sandwiches: whole grain bread, lettuce and tomato

For wraps: whole wheat wrap, lettuce and tomato

For toast: whole grain bread

For salad: baby spinach salad mix and homemade lemon tahini dressing (page 80)

1. In a large bowl, using a potato masher or the back of a fork, mash the chickpeas until about three-quarters of the chickpeas are mashed and the rest are left whole. Be mindful not to mash everything smooth; some bigger chunks make for the best texture.

2. Add the celery, bell pepper, apple, red onion, mayonnaise, Dijon mustard, dill, lemon juice, garlic powder, salt and pepper to the bowl and stir them well to combine. If you would prefer to use a food processor, add the celery, bell pepper, apple and chickpeas, and pulse until they're chopped into 1-inch (2.5-cm) chunks. Remove the ingredients from the food processor, and add them to a large bowl to mix in the remaining ingredients (mayonnaise, Dijon mustard, dill, lemon juice, garlic powder, salt and pepper).

3. Serve the chickpea mash in a sandwich, wrap, open-faced on toast or in a salad. Store leftovers in an airtight container in the fridge for 3 to 4 days.

RECIPE NOTES: Feel free to adjust the vegetable and seasoning ratios as you like! This is also great with chopped broccoli florets or diced carrot.

15-MINUTE SUN-DRIED TOMATOES & WHITE BEANS

Sometimes we just need a meal that can come together in 15 minutes, am I right? I rely on these Sun-dried Tomatoes & White Beans for those days when I really don't feel like cooking, and the best part about them is they only require one pot and a few pantry staples! The rich flavors of the sun-dried tomatoes pair perfectly with the white beans to create a protein-packed meal that's delicious on its own or served on toast or on crackers.

1. In a large pan over medium heat, heat the olive oil. Add the white beans, tomato paste, sun-dried tomatoes, tomato sauce, garlic powder, oregano, rosemary, maple syrup, salt and pepper. Sauté for 10 minutes or until the beans are warmed through.

2. Add the lemon juice and stir to combine everything. Serve it on toast, with crackers or on its own.

RECIPE NOTE: I used cannellini beans in this recipe, but navy beans, white kidney beans or chickpeas would also work well.

GOOD SOURCE OF PROTEIN, 15-MINUTE MEAL

SERVES 4

PREP: 5 MINUTES
COOK: 10 MINUTES
TOTAL: 15 MINUTES

1 tsp olive oil

1 (19-oz [540-g]) can white beans, drained and rinsed

1 (5½-oz [156-ml]) can tomato paste

¼ cup (14 g) sliced sun-dried tomatoes

½ cup (120 ml) tomato sauce

½ tsp garlic powder

½ tsp oregano

½ tsp rosemary

½ tsp maple syrup or other liquid sweetener

¼ tsp salt, or to taste

¼ tsp pepper

2 tbsp (30 ml) freshly squeezed lemon juice, about ½ lemon

Toast or crackers, optional

SERVES 3

PREP: 5–10 MINUTES
COOK: 20–25 MINUTES
TOTAL: 25–35 MINUTES

6½ oz (184 g) soba noodles

FOR THE GARLIC TOFU

1 (12-oz [350-g]) block
extra firm tofu, diced
1 tbsp (15 ml) olive oil
1 tsp garlic powder
¼ tsp salt

FOR THE PEANUT
MISO SAUCE

⅓ cup + 1 tbsp (95 g) natural
peanut butter
1½ tsp (8 g) white miso paste
1 tbsp (15 ml) maple syrup
¾ tbsp (11 ml) sesame oil
¾ tbsp (11 ml) soy sauce
1 tsp sriracha
1 tbsp (5 g) minced fresh
ginger
1 clove garlic, minced
2 tbsp (30 ml) lime juice,
about 1 lime
3 tbsp (45 ml) water or
plant-based milk (I used
unsweetened oat milk),
plus more as needed

FOR SERVING

1 bell pepper, sliced
1 cucumber, sliced
1 carrot, peeled

PEANUT-MISO TOFU NOODLE BOWL

For those nights when you're craving takeout but want something a little more nutritious and cost-effective, this Peanut-Miso Tofu Noodle Bowl is perfect. The combination of peanut butter and miso paste makes a super satisfying sauce that pairs perfectly with the garlic tofu and soba noodles. This recipe is intended to be eaten cold, but you could also replace the cucumber with bok choy and heat it up in a pan for a warming, comforting meal. If you don't have soba noodles on hand, rice noodles would also work perfectly.

1. Preheat the oven to 450°F (232°C) and line a baking sheet with parchment paper.

2. In a large bowl, toss together the tofu, olive oil, garlic powder and salt for the garlic tofu. Spread the mixture evenly on the baking sheet and bake for 20 to 25 minutes, or until the tofu is lightly golden brown, flipping halfway through.

3. Cook your soba noodles as per package instructions.

4. Meanwhile, whisk or blend together the peanut butter, miso paste, maple syrup, sesame oil, soy sauce, sriracha, ginger, garlic, lime juice and water for the peanut miso sauce. Feel free to add water or plant-based milk for the sauce, 1 tablespoon (15 ml) at a time, to reach your desired consistency. If the sauce is too thick, add more water or milk as needed.

5. Once the garlic tofu and peanut miso sauce are complete, mix them together in a large bowl with the noodles, bell pepper, cucumber and carrot if you're serving it cold, or add everything to a large pan over medium heat to warm it.

6. Refrigerate leftovers in an airtight container for up to 5 days.

RECIPE NOTE: Feel free to add more sriracha if you'd like it spicier!

SPICY CREAMY FUSILLI PASTA

GOOD SOURCE
OF IRON,
30-MINUTE MEAL

I created this fusilli pasta on a whim one evening when recipe testing. I wanted to create a pasta recipe that could be your go-to when you don't have many ingredients on hand and need dinner, like, *immediately*. I was surprised that a pasta that was so simple could turn out to be so flavorful, but the garlic, chili flakes, tomato paste and plant-based milk really work together to make a beautiful, spicy flavor and a creamy texture. My brother, who isn't plant-based, told me that this was his favorite recipe I've ever made. And I think it's one of mine, too!

SERVES 3

PREP: 5 MINUTES
COOK: 25 MINUTES
TOTAL: 30 MINUTES

1. In a large pan over medium heat, sauté the onion in olive oil and salt for 4 to 5 minutes, until the onion is translucent.

2. Meanwhile, cook the pasta in well-salted water as per the package instructions. Reserve ¼ cup (60 ml) of the pasta water before draining.

3. Add the garlic and chili flakes to the pan with the onion and sauté them for 2 to 3 minutes, until the garlic is lightly golden brown but not burnt.

4. Add the tomato paste and mix to combine it. Pour in the plant-based milk and mix until well combined. Continue to sauté the mixture until it has heated through.

5. Add the lentils, kale and pasta. Sauté everything until the lentils are heated through and the kale has wilted. Add the pasta water if needed to moisten the mixture, about 1 tbsp (15 ml) at a time until you reach the desired consistency.

6. Refrigerate any leftovers in an airtight container for up to 4 days.

1 yellow onion, diced

1 tbsp (15 ml) olive oil

¼ tsp salt, plus 1 tsp for the pasta water

11 oz (300 g) fusilli pasta

5 cloves garlic, minced

1 tsp chili flakes
(see Recipe Notes)

1 (5½-oz [156-ml]) can tomato paste

¾ cup (180 ml) plant-based milk (I used unsweetened oat milk)

½ (19-oz [540-g]) can lentils, drained and rinsed

1 cup (67 g) chopped kale

RECIPE NOTES: If you want a completely smooth sauce, blend the sauce in a blender after cooking to get rid of the chunks of onion.

For a less spicy or kid-friendly pasta, I recommend halving the amount of chili flakes or leaving them out.

SERVES 4

PREP: 5 MINUTES
COOK: 20 MINUTES
· TOTAL: 25 MINUTES

FOR THE TEMPEH
"BACON"

1½ cups (360 ml) no-salt-added vegetable stock

1 tbsp (15 ml) olive oil

1 tbsp (15 ml) maple syrup or other sugar

1 tbsp (15 ml) + 1 tsp soy sauce

½ tsp liquid smoke

1 tsp smoked paprika

1 tsp garlic powder

1 (9-oz [250-g]) package tempeh, sliced into 16 (½-inch [1.3-cm]) strips

FOR ASSEMBLY

8 slices whole wheat bread

½ cup (120 ml) vegan mayonnaise

2 large on-the-vine tomatoes, thinly sliced

8 romaine leaves, about 1 head

Salt and pepper, to taste

VEGAN TEMPEH BLT SANDWICH

Growing up, one of my favorite meals was a BLT sandwich. When I became vegan, I set out to recreate my beloved BLT with plant-based ingredients so I wouldn't have to live without it, and I think this tempeh BLT is pretty close to the real thing. This recipe uses liquid smoke, an ingredient found in barbecue sauce and smoked meats, which gives it the quintessential smoky flavor. It can be found in the spice or barbecue sauce aisle of most grocery stores, but if you don't have any on hand, you'll still achieve a bit of the smoky flavor from the smoked paprika. I love this recipe because you can make the tempeh ahead of time, so all you have to do is throw together the other sandwich ingredients for a quick and easy meal throughout the week!

1. To a blender, add the vegetable stock, olive oil, maple syrup, soy sauce, liquid smoke, smoked paprika and garlic powder, and blend until it's well combined. You can also whisk the ingredients together if you prefer.

2. In a large pan over medium heat, lay the tempeh strips evenly and pour the marinade over them, making sure they're evenly covered. Raise the heat to high to bring the liquid to a low boil. Then reduce the heat to low-medium, continuing to simmer the tempeh and letting the liquid reduce. This should take about 15 minutes. Flip the tempeh every 3 to 4 minutes, until all the marinade has soaked into the tempeh.

3. Once the tempeh is cooked, assemble the sandwiches. Toast your bread and spread each slice with 1 tablespoon (15 ml) of vegan mayonnaise. Add 4 slices of tempeh, a few slices of tomato and 2 romaine leaves to each sandwich. Add some salt and pepper to taste and enjoy.

4. Refrigerate tempeh leftovers in an airtight container for up to 5 days.

RECIPE NOTES: Tempeh is made by fermenting soy beans, then forming them together into blocks. It's a great source of protein, iron, calcium and probiotics. If you've never had it before, it has a slightly nutty, earthy fermented flavor. Don't knock it 'til you try it!

Most tempeh recipes require steaming the tempeh, then marinating it to reduce some of the bitterness and allow as much of the marinade to absorb as possible. I've combined these two steps in this recipe by steaming the tempeh in the marinade to make the process a bit faster.

SERVES 3

PREP: 15 MINUTES
COOK: 20 MINUTES
TOTAL: 35 MINUTES

FOR THE LENTIL "MEATBALLS"

1 yellow onion, diced

2 tbsp (30 ml) olive oil, divided

4 cloves garlic, minced

¼ cup (20 g) large flake oats

⅔ cup (60 g) oat flour, plus 2 tbsp (10 g) as needed

¼ cup (15 g) fresh Italian parsley, packed

1 cup (198 g) cooked lentils (I used canned brown lentils, drained and rinsed)

1 tbsp (6 g) Italian seasoning

2 tbsp (22 g) nutritional yeast

1 tbsp (14 g) tomato paste

1 tbsp (10 g) chia seeds

¾ tsp salt

¼ tsp pepper

HERBY LENTIL "MEATBALLS" & GARLIC BREAD

If you think you don't like lentils, try this recipe and see if it changes your mind. The lentil meatballs are bursting with earthy flavors from the Italian herbs and parsley, while the marinara sauce is perfect for dipping the warm, flavorful garlic bread. Originally, I thought this would be a red sauce pasta recipe, but I fell in love with the idea of serving the lentil meatballs with warm garlic bread to dip in the marinara sauce. The meatballs offer a great dose of plant-based protein and iron, making this dish super satisfying. Of course, you can still serve this recipe with pasta if you'd like, but I think it's hearty and filling enough on its own. This recipe may look complicated, but I promise that it's very straightforward and can easily be a weeknight dinner staple!

1. Preheat the oven to 400°F (204°C). Line two baking sheets with parchment paper.

2. To begin the lentil "meatballs," in a small pan over medium heat, sauté the onion in 1 tablespoon (15 ml) of olive oil until it's translucent, 3 to 4 minutes. Add the garlic to the pan about 2 minutes in, being careful not to burn it.

3. Add the sautéed onion and garlic to a large blender or food processor with the oats, oat flour, Italian parsley, lentils, Italian seasoning, nutritional yeast, tomato paste, chia seeds, salt, pepper and the remaining 1 tablespoon (15 ml) of olive oil. Blend them until the ingredients are well combined together, but not puréed. This took me about 15 seconds in my high-speed blender.

4. Once the ingredients are well combined, assess the texture. The lentil meatballs should be the consistency of cookie dough: moist and easy to form into balls, but not too wet or dry. Add water or more oat flour 1 tablespoon (6 g) at a time to achieve the desired consistency, if needed.

5. With wet hands to keep the dough from sticking to you, form the dough into balls, with about 2 tablespoons (18 g) of dough in each ball. You should have approximately 12 lentil meatballs.

6. Place the lentil meatballs on a baking sheet and bake them for 20 to 25 minutes, flipping halfway through, until the lentil meatballs are golden brown and have firmed up.

7. Meanwhile, for the garlic bread, cut the baguette in half, then cut it again in half lengthwise. In a small bowl, mix together the vegan butter, garlic, parsley, garlic powder and salt. Spread the mixture on both sides of the baguette. You may have some garlic butter left over.

8. Place the garlic bread on a baking sheet, and once the meatballs have been cooking for about 10 minutes, add the garlic bread to the oven, too. Bake it for 10 to 15 minutes, until the edges are golden brown.

9. Meanwhile, in the same pan you sautéed the onion and garlic in, gently heat the marinara sauce over low-medium heat. Once the meatballs are golden brown, remove them from the oven and add them to the marinara sauce, mixing to coat the meatballs.

10. Serve the lentil meatballs and marinara with the garlic bread on the side to dip.

11. The garlic bread is best eaten fresh. Refrigerate any lentil meatball leftovers for up to 4 days.

FOR THE GARLIC BREAD

½ **large baguette**

⅓ **cup (80 g) vegan butter**

1 **clove garlic, minced**

1 **tbsp (4 g) fresh Italian parsley, minced**

1 **tsp garlic powder**

⅛ **tsp salt**

ADDITIONAL INGREDIENTS

2 **cups (480 ml) marinara sauce**

EASY BROCCOLI & BOK CHOY NOODLES

My partner and I came up with this recipe when we didn't have many fresh ingredients on hand. We had a block of tofu, bok choy and some frozen broccoli in the freezer. Frozen fruit and veggies often get a bad rap, which is too bad because they're convenient and just as nutritious as fresh! Not to mention they can be *way* more budget friendly, especially if you live in a cold climate like I do where fruit and veggies don't flourish all year round! I love this recipe because you can steam the veggies, cook the buckwheat noodles and whisk the sauce together while the garlic tofu is cooking, making it come together super quickly. Plus, you can totally customize the sauce based on your taste preferences. Feel free to use more or less lime for tanginess, sesame oil for nuttiness, soy sauce for saltiness and sriracha for spice.

1. Preheat the oven to 450°F (232°C) and line a baking sheet with parchment paper.

2. In a large bowl, toss together the tofu, olive oil, garlic powder and salt. Lay everything evenly on the baking sheet and bake for 20 minutes, or until the tofu is golden brown, flipping halfway through.

3. Meanwhile, steam the broccoli for 5 minutes. Once the broccoli is almost fork tender, add the bok choy to your steamer and cook for 2 to 3 minutes more.

4. Cook the buckwheat noodles as per package instructions.

5. Whisk together the lime juice, sesame oil, soy sauce and sriracha for the sauce.

6. Once all the components are complete, combine the tofu, sauce, noodles, broccoli and bok choy together in a large bowl and enjoy.

7. Refrigerate leftovers in an airtight container for up to 4 days.

RECIPE NOTES: When preparing bok choy, I recommend cutting off the bottom part that holds the stalks together. Wash the bok choy well, then slice the tougher stems into ½-inch (1.3-cm) chunks and leave the leafy green part whole.

I used buckwheat noodles in this recipe since they're a great source of protein and fiber, but I've also made this recipe with rice noodles and the bowl turns out equally delicious.

SERVES 4

PREP: 5 MINUTES
COOK: 20 MINUTES
TOTAL: 25 MINUTES

FOR THE TOFU
1 (12-oz [350-g]) block extra firm tofu, diced

1 tbsp (15 ml) olive oil

1 tsp garlic powder

¼ tsp salt

FOR ASSEMBLY
3 cups (273 g) broccoli florets

4 heads bok choy, sliced (see Recipe Notes)

9 oz (250 g) buckwheat noodles (see Recipe Notes)

FOR THE SAUCE
1 tbsp (15 ml) lime juice, about ½ lime, or to taste

2½ tbsp (37 ml) sesame oil, or to taste

2½ tbsp (37 ml) soy sauce, or to taste

2 tsp (10 ml) sriracha, or to taste

BARBECUE CHICKPEA WRAPS

SERVES 4

PREP: 5 MINUTES
COOK: 25 MINUTES
TOTAL: 30 MINUTES

FOR THE BARBECUE CHICKPEAS

1 (19-oz [540-g]) can chickpeas, drained and rinsed

1 tbsp (15 ml) olive oil

2 cloves garlic, minced

½ cup (120 ml) barbecue sauce

1 tbsp (15 ml) sriracha or other hot sauce

FOR ASSEMBLY

4 large whole wheat wraps

¼ cup (60 ml) vegan mayonnaise (see Recipe Notes)

2 cups (94 g) romaine, diced

1 cucumber, sliced

¼ red onion, diced

I have a confession: Lunch is my least favorite meal to make. Don't get me wrong, I love eating it, but there's something about the pressure of having to take time away from the work day to throw a meal together that just seems like a hassle. This is why I set out to create easy, delicious recipes, like these Barbecue Chickpea Wraps, that are pretty hands off and can be prepped ahead of time to make your lunches come together more seamlessly throughout the week. These wraps level up the classic, boring veggie sandwich by adding sweet and smoky barbecue-roasted chickpeas with crispy romaine, cucumber and onion. The result is a delicious wrap that can easily be thrown together in no time and will keep you powering through an afternoon of work or activities.

1. Preheat the oven to 400°F (204°C) and line a baking sheet with parchment paper.

2. To make the barbecue chickpeas, in a large bowl, combine the chickpeas, olive oil, garlic, barbecue sauce and sriracha, and stir well to combine. Lay the barbecue chickpeas on the baking sheet, ensuring they're evenly spaced so that they roast rather than steam.

3. Bake the chickpeas for 20 minutes, flipping halfway through, until the barbecue sauce has soaked into the chickpeas and they're slightly golden, being careful not to burn them.

4. Assemble your wrap by spreading it with 1 tablespoon (15 ml) of vegan mayonnaise, ½ cup (83 g) of the barbecue chickpeas, ½ cup (24 g) of romaine, ¼ of the sliced cucumber and 1 tablespoon (3 g) of diced red onion. Wrap and enjoy!

5. Refrigerate leftover barbecue chickpeas in an airtight container for up to 5 days.

RECIPE NOTES: If you don't have vegan mayonnaise on hand, feel free to use hummus instead.

It's important to remember to flip the chickpeas halfway through cooking, or else the barbecue sauce may burn.

If you'd like the chickpeas to be crispier, feel free to roast them at 450°F (232°C) for 25 to 30 minutes, making sure to flip the chickpeas every 7 minutes.

SMOKY BLACK BEAN CHILI

There's something about a delicious, hearty chili during the winter that just feels so right. This Smoky Black Bean Chili is the perfect cozy, comforting dish while still being packed with plant-based protein, fiber and tons of veggies. I decided to add quinoa to this chili recipe to make it a bit heartier and more filling, and the texture works so well with the beans and vegetables. It has a bit of a kick to it from the chipotle peppers, so feel free to reduce the amount if you don't like spicy food. I'd argue that this chili tastes even better the next day, making it the perfect meal to prep ahead of time to eat throughout the week.

SERVES 6

PREP: 10 MINUTES
COOK: 45 MINUTES
TOTAL: 55 MINUTES

1. In a large pot over medium heat, sauté the onion with the olive oil until it is translucent, 4 to 5 minutes.

2. Add the garlic, carrots, bell pepper, mushrooms, chipotle peppers, chili powder, smoked paprika, chili flakes, salt and pepper. Sauté them for an additional 4 to 5 minutes, until the water from the mushrooms has released and evaporated.

3. Add the black beans, diced tomatoes, crushed tomatoes, vegetable stock and quinoa. Stir to combine, and increase the heat to medium-high to bring the chili to a simmer, 5 to 10 minutes. Once it's simmering, add the lid to the pot and reduce the heat to low-medium.

4. Let the chili simmer for 30 to 35 minutes, stirring occasionally, or until the quinoa is fully cooked and the carrots are fork tender.

5. Serve garnished with the lime juice, fresh cilantro, vegan cheese and corn chips, if using, and enjoy!

6. Refrigerate leftovers in an airtight container for up to 5 days.

RECIPE NOTE: This is a thick, hearty chili recipe. If you prefer a thinner consistency, feel free to add another 1 to 2 cups (240 to 480 ml) of vegetable stock while simmering.

FOR THE CHILI

1 yellow onion, diced

1 tbsp (15 ml) olive oil

4 cloves garlic, minced

2 cups (256 g) carrots, quartered and diced

1 large orange bell pepper, diced

16 oz (454 g) cremini mushrooms, sliced

2–3 chipotle peppers in adobo sauce, diced

2 tbsp (20 g) chili powder

2 tsp (6 g) smoked paprika

¼ tsp chili flakes

1½ tsp (9 g) salt

¼ tsp pepper

2 (19-oz [540-g]) cans black beans, drained and rinsed

1 (28-oz [796-ml]) can no-salt-added diced tomatoes

1 (28-oz [796-ml]) can crushed tomatoes

1½ cups (360 ml) no-salt-added vegetable stock (see Recipe Note)

¾ cup (139 g) uncooked quinoa

OPTIONAL TOPPINGS

Lime juice

Fresh cilantro

Vegan cheese

Corn chips

ONE-PAN MUSHROOM GNOCCHI

12 oz (340 g) cremini mushrooms, sliced

4 cloves garlic, minced

2 tbsp (30 ml) olive oil, divided

18 oz (510 g) gnocchi

½ tsp salt, or to taste

¼ tsp pepper, or to taste

1 cup (240 ml) no-salt-added vegetable stock

½ (19-oz [540-g]) can cannellini beans, drained and rinsed (see Recipe Notes)

2 cups (134 g) thinly sliced kale

3 tbsp (33 g) nutritional yeast, or to taste

2–4 tbsp (30–60 ml) lemon juice, ½–1 lemon, to taste

One-pan dishes are a lifesaver when I don't really feel like cooking or doing the dishes (okay, I pretty much never feel like doing the dishes). This One-Pan Mushroom Gnocchi uses mostly pantry staples, meaning it comes together quickly while still being well-balanced. One of my secrets for making a pasta dish more nutritious is adding white beans. They're mild in flavor, creamy and add a good dose of protein and fiber. Plus, if you use canned beans, it's as easy as opening up the can and adding the beans near the end of the cooking time. This may look like a lot of mushrooms when you're cooking them, but they wilt down so much that it ends up being the perfect amount. Try out this gnocchi dish when you're craving something easy and nourishing that's still packed with flavor!

1. In a large pan over medium heat, sauté the mushrooms and garlic in 1 tablespoon (15 ml) of olive oil for 5 to 10 minutes, until the water has released and evaporated from the mushrooms.

2. Add the gnocchi, salt, pepper and remaining tablespoon (15 ml) of olive oil to the pan, and sauté for 3 minutes with the lid on. You'll notice that the gnocchi will begin to brown and crisp up.

3. Add the vegetable stock and use your spoon to scrape the brown bits from the bottom of the pan. Sauté for an additional 5 minutes with the lid off.

4. Add the cannellini beans, kale, nutritional yeast and lemon juice, and sauté for another 3 to 4 minutes, until the kale has wilted.

5. Refrigerate leftovers in an airtight container for up to 4 days.

RECIPE NOTES: I encourage you to season this gnocchi recipe based on your personal taste preferences. Add more lemon juice for a brighter, tangier flavor, more salt or pepper for more seasoning or more nutritional yeast for a cheesy, savory flavor.

Most grocery stores carry a variety of canned white beans, such as cannellini beans, white navy beans and white beans. Any of these options will work!

WARMING
SOUPS

There's very little I love more than a good soup. I have fond memories of coming back from a day of skiing with my family to a big bowl of stew, and my partner and I often rely on soups as easy weeknight meals throughout the colder months since they're so easy to throw together. Even outside of the winter season, I could happily eat soup every single night for dinner and never get bored, so having a variety of delicious soup recipes on hand, like my Creamy Tomato Basil Soup (page 59), is vital.

If you find that soups don't leave you feeling satisfied, I recommend making sure that you're adding a good source of protein, carbs, fat and fiber to the soup. This could look like using beans or lentils for protein and fiber, adding some potatoes or serving with a slice of bread for carbohydrates and using olive oil or blended nuts or seeds in the soup for creaminess. I love that these recipes provide a great source of veggies when salads don't sound very appetizing and that most are one-pot, which means quick cooking and even quicker clean up!

My Nourishing Curry Lentil Stew (page 55) is perfect for when I need something extra wholesome, while my Hearty Vegan Sausage Stew (page 60) is a stick-to-your-ribs option. If you have plant-based skeptics in your household, try making them the Spicy Black Bean Tortilla Soup (page 56), and I promise they'll be convinced. You can even make these recipes ahead of a busy week to have a quick and delicious lunch or dinner option prepped ahead of time!

NOURISHING CURRY LENTIL STEW

If you're looking for the ultimate cozy, warming stew, this is it. It's the perfect weeknight dinner recipe since it uses mostly canned ingredients, only takes a few minutes to throw together and has a great balance of plant-based protein, fiber and fat to keep you feeling full. Incorporating lentils into our meals is a great way to help make sure we're getting enough plant-based iron, and the vitamin C from the diced tomatoes helps to increase iron absorption. This stew has a mild curry flavor that pairs perfectly with the creamy coconut milk.

1. In a large pot over medium heat, sauté the onion and garlic in the olive oil until the onion is translucent, 3 to 4 minutes. Add the carrots, sweet potato, tomatoes, curry powder, chili flakes, if using, salt and pepper. Stir to combine.

2. Add the lentils, coconut milk and vegetable stock. Stir to combine everything, cover the pot and increase the heat to high to bring the soup to a boil. Once the soup is boiling, reduce the heat to low and let it simmer for 20 to 25 minutes, until the sweet potato is fork tender.

3. Transfer half of the soup (about 4 cups [960 ml]) to a high-speed blender and blend until smooth. Add the blended soup back into the pot with the rest of the soup. Add the spinach and let it wilt for about 2 minutes. Serve and enjoy.

4. Leftovers can be stored in an airtight container in the fridge for up to 4 days.

RECIPE NOTES: Adjust the curry powder, chili flakes and salt as per your taste buds!

If you prefer a thinner soup, feel free to omit blending the soup.

GOOD SOURCE OF PROTEIN AND IRON

SERVES 6

PREP: 10 MINUTES
COOK: 25–30 MINUTES
TOTAL: 35–40 MINUTES

1 yellow onion, diced

3 cloves garlic, minced

1 tbsp (15 ml) olive oil

1 cup (128 g) diced carrots

1 medium sweet potato, diced

1 (28-oz [796-ml]) can no-salt-added diced tomatoes

1 tbsp (10 g) curry powder

½ tsp chili flakes, optional

1 tsp salt

¼ tsp pepper

2 (19-oz [540-g]) cans lentils, drained and rinsed

1 (14-oz [400-ml]) can coconut milk

4 cups (960 ml) no-salt-added vegetable stock

3 cups spinach (90 g) or kale (201 g)

SERVES 5

PREP: 5 MINUTES
COOK: 30 MINUTES
TOTAL: 35 MINUTES

1 yellow onion, diced

2 tbsp (30 ml) olive oil, divided

3 cloves garlic, minced

2 chipotle peppers in adobo sauce, finely chopped

1 orange bell pepper, diced

1 (19-oz [540-g]) can black beans, drained and rinsed

1 (12-oz [340-g]) can whole kernel corn, drained

1 (28-oz [796-ml]) can no-salt-added diced tomatoes

3 cups (720 ml) no-salt-added vegetable stock

2 tsp (6 g) chili powder

½ tsp cumin

1 (5½-oz [156-ml]) can tomato paste

1½ tsp (9 g) salt

¼ tsp pepper

5 small flour or corn tortillas (see Recipe Note)

1 tbsp (15 ml) lime juice, about ½ lime

OPTIONAL TOPPINGS
Fresh cilantro, chopped
Fresh lime juice
Vegan cheese
Vegan sour cream

SPICY BLACK BEAN TORTILLA SOUP

Some recipes take me a few tries to get right, and others come together so well on the first try that it feels like fate. That's what happened with this Spicy Black Bean Tortilla Soup. The flavors of this soup completely blew me away, and the additional toppings added at the end elevated it even further. I love that this soup uses black beans as the main protein source since they're high in fiber and plant-based iron. The vitamin C from the bell pepper, tomatoes and lime juice help to increase the absorption of the iron, making this a super nutritious meal!

1. In a large pot over medium heat, sauté the onion in 1 tablespoon (15 ml) of olive oil until the onion is translucent, 4 to 5 minutes. Add the garlic and chipotle peppers, and sauté them for another 2 to 3 minutes.

2. Stir in the bell pepper, black beans, corn, diced tomatoes, vegetable stock, chili powder, cumin, tomato paste, salt and pepper. Increase the heat to medium-high for 5 to 10 minutes to bring the soup to a boil, and when it starts to bubble, reduce the heat back to low and simmer for 20 minutes.

3. Meanwhile, add the remaining 1 tablespoon (15 ml) of olive oil to a large pan, and fry the tortillas over low heat for 3 to 4 minutes on each side, until they've crisped up and are lightly golden brown.

4. Once the soup is done, add the lime juice. Slice the tortillas into long strips, and use them to top the soup, alongside the other optional toppings to serve.

RECIPE NOTE: If you don't have tortillas on hand, feel free to use tortilla chips instead to top the soup.

CREAMY TOMATO BASIL SOUP

ONE-POT MEAL,
30-MINUTE MEAL

SERVES 6

PREP: 5 MINUTES
COOK: 20 MINUTES
TOTAL: 25 MINUTES

Is there anything more comforting than a creamy tomato soup? This Creamy Tomato Basil Soup is the best plant-based tomato soup I've ever eaten, plus it's super easy and actually provides a great dose of plant-based protein. The secret ingredient? White beans! I love adding white beans to my blended soups since you can't even taste them, and they add plant-based protein, fiber and iron. This soup also uses coconut milk to make it creamy, but I promise it doesn't taste like coconut. It also comes together in less than 30 minutes and requires almost no chopping. I can pretty much guarantee this soup will become one of your new favorite recipes!

1 yellow onion, diced

1 tbsp (15 ml) olive oil

1–1½ tsp (6–9 g) salt, or to taste

¼ tsp pepper

4 cloves garlic, minced

1 tsp dried oregano

1 tsp dried thyme

2 (28-oz [796-ml]) cans no-salt-added diced tomatoes

1 (14-oz [400-ml]) can full-fat coconut milk

3 cups (720 ml) no-salt-added vegetable stock

1 (19-oz [540-g]) can white beans, drained and rinsed

1 bunch (25 g) fresh basil leaves, sliced

1. In a large pot over medium heat, sauté the onion with the olive oil, salt and pepper until the onion is translucent, 3 to 4 minutes.

2. Add the garlic, oregano and thyme, and sauté until the garlic starts to become golden brown, 2 to 3 minutes, being careful that it doesn't burn.

3. Add the diced tomatoes, coconut milk and vegetable stock, and increase the temperature to medium-high to bring the soup to a low boil. Cover it with a lid, reduce the heat to low-medium and let it simmer for 10 minutes, stirring occasionally.

4. Add the soup to a high-speed blender with the white beans and blend until it's smooth. You could also use an immersion blender at this step instead.

5. If you're using a high-speed blender, add the soup back into the pot and bring it to a low simmer to heat it through. Add the fresh basil, stir to let it wilt for 1 to 2 minutes and enjoy.

6. Refrigerate leftovers in an airtight container for up to 5 days.

RECIPE NOTES: One of the biggest tips I can give you when cooking is to taste as you go. Soups are meant to be relatively salty, which is why this one has 1½ teaspoons (9 g) of salt, but feel free to start with ¾ teaspoon and add more as needed.

I rely on no-salt-added vegetable stock and diced tomatoes in most of my recipes because this gives me more control over the salt content. If your vegetable stock or diced tomatoes have added salt, I recommend you reduce the amount of salt you add to the recipe.

SERVES 4

PREP: 10 MINUTES
COOK: 25–30 MINUTES
TOTAL: 35–40 MINUTES

1 yellow onion, diced

1 tbsp (15 ml) olive oil

4 cloves garlic, minced

3 stalks celery, diced

2 large carrots, diced

2 medium yellow potatoes,
diced (see Recipe Notes)

3 spicy vegan sausages, sliced
(I used Beyond Meat Hot
Italian Sausages; see Recipe
Notes)

1 tsp dried thyme

1 tsp dried rosemary

1¼ tsp (8 g) salt

¾ tsp pepper

1 (5½-oz [156-ml]) can
tomato paste

6 cups (1.4 L) no-salt-added
vegetable stock

1 bay leaf

1 tbsp (15 ml) balsamic vinegar

2 cups (134 g) kale,
destemmed and sliced

HEARTY VEGAN SAUSAGE STEW

I chose not to create many recipes that use vegan meat alternatives in this book, but I felt like I needed one super hearty, meaty stew that would turn even the biggest plant-based skeptics into believers. This Hearty Vegan Sausage Stew uses potatoes, carrots, celery and vegan sausage to create a stick-to-your-ribs type of stew, and I even added a splash of balsamic vinegar to add an unexpected depth of flavor. If you feel like stew never leaves you feeling full or satisfied, I urge you to try this recipe. This is one of my favorite stews I've ever made, so I hope you like it, too!

1. In a large pot over medium heat, sauté the onion in the olive oil until the onion is translucent, 4 to 5 minutes.

2. Add the garlic, celery, carrots, potatoes, vegan sausages, thyme, rosemary, salt and pepper. Sauté for another 2 to 3 minutes, until the rosemary and thyme are fragrant.

3. Add the tomato paste, vegetable stock and bay leaf. Stir to combine everything. Increase the heat to medium-high to bring the soup to a low boil, then reduce it back to medium heat, place a lid on the pot and simmer the soup for 20 to 25 minutes, or until the potatoes are fork tender.

4. Remove the bay leaf and add the balsamic vinegar and kale. Continue to simmer for 2 to 3 more minutes, or until the kale is wilted.

5. Refrigerate leftovers in an airtight container for up to 4 days.

RECIPE NOTES: I chose not to peel the potatoes to keep the extra fiber and nutrients, but feel free to peel them if you'd prefer.

Most grocery stores will have a plant-based section with some sort of vegan sausages. It doesn't make a huge difference which type you buy since they're cooked in the stew with other flavorings, but I think spicy Italian vegan sausages work well.

GARLICKY WHITE BEAN SOUP & HOMEMADE CROUTONS

One of the most common questions I get as a plant-based dietitian and recipe developer is how to make plant-based soups, sauces and pastas creamy. Sunflower seeds are one of my all-time favorite ways to achieve a creamy texture without having to use any dairy. While many plant-based recipes rely on cashews for creaminess, I've found over the years that sunflower seeds work just as well, are higher in protein and are typically much more budget friendly than cashews. This Garlicky White Bean Soup includes celery, carrots, plenty of garlic, thyme and nutritional yeast for delicious flavor. We top it all off with super easy homemade garlic croutons, which are optional but definitely recommended.

1. Preheat the oven to 375°F (190°C) and line a baking sheet with parchment paper.

2. To begin the soup, in a large pot over medium heat, sauté the onion, celery, carrots and garlic in olive oil until the onion is translucent, 3 to 4 minutes. Add the vegetable stock, salt, pepper and thyme, and bring the soup to a simmer for 10 to 12 minutes with the lid on, until the carrots are fork tender.

3. Add the contents of the pot to a high-speed blender with the sunflower seeds and white beans. Blend until it's super smooth.

4. Add the soup back into the pot. Increase the heat to medium-high to bring the soup to a low boil. Add the lid and reduce the heat back down to low to simmer for 10 minutes.

5. Meanwhile, make the croutons. Add the baguette, olive oil, garlic powder and salt to a large bowl and toss to combine. Add the croutons to the baking sheet and bake for 10 to 15 minutes, flipping halfway through, until the croutons are golden brown.

6. Add the nutritional yeast and lemon juice to the soup.

7. Top the soup with the croutons and toppings, if using, serve and enjoy.

8. Refrigerate any leftover soup in an airtight container for up to 5 days. Store the croutons separately at room temperature for up to 3 days.

> RECIPE NOTES: An immersion blender would also work well to blend the soup; just make sure your carrots are soft enough.

GOOD SOURCE OF PROTEIN AND IRON

SERVES 3

PREP: 10 MINUTES
COOK: 25 MINUTES
TOTAL: 35 MINUTES

FOR THE SOUP

1 yellow onion, diced

3 stalks celery, diced

3 large carrots, diced

5 cloves garlic, minced

1 tbsp (15 ml) olive oil

4 cups (960 ml) no-salt-added vegetable stock

1¼ tsp (8 g) salt, or to taste

¼ tsp pepper

1 tsp dried thyme

¼ cup (33 g) raw, hulled, unsalted sunflower seeds

1 (19-oz [540-g]) can white beans, drained and rinsed

3 tbsp (33 g) nutritional yeast

¼ cup (60 ml) lemon juice, about 1 lemon

FOR THE CROUTONS

½ baguette, cut or torn into small pieces

½ tbsp (7 ml) olive oil

¼ tsp garlic powder

¼ tsp salt

OPTIONAL TOPPINGS

Fresh chopped parsley

Fresh squeezed lemon

Pepper

ONE-POT MEAL

SERVES 4

PREP: 10 MINUTES
COOK: 25–30 MINUTES
TOTAL: 35–40 MINUTES

FOR THE SOUP
1 yellow onion, diced
3 celery stalks, diced
3 large carrots, diced
1 tbsp (15 ml) olive oil
4 cloves garlic, minced
1 tsp dried thyme
1 tsp dried oregano
1 tsp dried parsley
2 medium yellow potatoes, diced
2 tbsp (16 g) all-purpose flour
1 tsp salt, or to taste
½ tsp pepper, or to taste
6 cups (1.4 L) no-salt-added vegetable stock
1 dried bay leaf
1 (19-oz [540-g]) can white beans, drained and rinsed

FOR THE DUMPLINGS
2 cups (240 g) all-purpose flour
1 tsp baking soda
½ tsp dried oregano
½ tsp parsley
½ tsp salt
½ cup (120 ml) warm water
2 tbsp (30 ml) olive oil

BROTHY VEGETABLE DUMPLING SOUP

Growing up, my brothers and I used to love chicken dumpling soup that came in a can. I can't promise that the soup was actually very good, but eating it with my brothers is a core memory for me. I set out to create a more nourishing, plant-based version of the dumpling soup that I loved so much, and I have to admit that I think this one is way more delicious. If you've never made dumpling soup before, don't worry—it's super easy to make and requires just a few simple ingredients you probably already have in your fridge and pantry!

1. To begin the soup, in a large pot over medium heat, sauté the onion, celery and carrots in olive oil until the onion is translucent, 3 to 4 minutes.

2. Add the garlic, thyme, oregano, parsley, potatoes, flour, salt and pepper, and sauté them for another 2 to 3 minutes.

3. Add the vegetable stock, bay leaf and white beans. Increase the heat to medium-high, bringing the soup to a simmer. Add the lid and reduce the heat back down to low. Let the soup simmer for 7 minutes.

4. Meanwhile, in a large bowl, whisk together the flour, baking soda, oregano, parsley and salt for the dumplings. In a separate small bowl, combine the warm water and olive oil. Pour the warm water and olive oil into the flour mixture and stir to combine. It should look like bread dough, neither too wet nor too dry.

5. After the soup has been simmering for 10 minutes, using a spoon, drop the dumpling dough into the soup in small, approximately 1 tablespoon-sized (15-g) balls. Let them cook in the soup for 15 to 20 minutes with the lid on, or until the dumplings are cooked through, ensuring the potatoes are fork tender. Remove the bay leaf.

6. This soup is best served immediately.

7. Leftovers can be refrigerated in an airtight container for up to 3 days, but the dumplings may become soggy.

RECIPE NOTE: The dumpling dough should be moist but not runny. Feel free to add additional flour or water if needed.

PEANUT CURRY NOODLE SOUP

I've been making curry-inspired noodle soup for years, so I knew I wanted to include a similar version of it in this cookbook but elevated with the addition of peanut butter. I love this recipe because the nutty, creamy flavors from the coconut milk and peanut butter pair so perfectly with the earthiness from the mushrooms and spice of the curry powder. I encourage you to taste as you go and add additional lime, soy sauce, sesame oil, chili flakes or chopped peanuts as desired. This soup is so easy to whip up on those days you know you need something warming and filling but don't want to spend forever cooking.

1. In a large pot over medium heat, sauté the shallot in olive oil until it's translucent, 3 to 4 minutes.

2. Add the ginger, garlic and mushrooms. Sauté them for another 3 to 4 minutes, until the water has released and evaporated from the mushrooms.

3. Meanwhile, in a large bowl, whisk together the vegetable stock, peanut butter and miso paste.

4. Add the curry powder, salt and chili flakes to the pot and sauté to combine. Pour in the vegetable stock and peanut butter mixture, coconut milk, soy sauce, sesame oil and tofu. Increase the heat to medium-high to bring the mixture to a low boil, then add the lid and reduce the heat to low to let it simmer for 10 minutes.

5. Meanwhile, cook the buckwheat noodles as per the package instructions.

6. Add the rice vinegar, lime juice and bok choy to the pot with the soup. Cook for 2 to 3 minutes more, until the bok choy is wilted. To serve, place the buckwheat noodles in a bowl and pour the soup on top. Feel free to add any additional toppings to serve.

7. Refrigerate the buckwheat noodles and soup separately in airtight containers for up to 4 days.

30-MINUTE MEAL

SERVES 4

PREP: 5 MINUTES
COOK: 20 MINUTES
TOTAL: 25 MINUTES

FOR THE SOUP

1 shallot, sliced

1 tbsp (15 ml) olive oil

2 tbsp (10 g) minced fresh ginger

3 cloves garlic, minced

16 oz (454 g) cremini mushrooms, sliced

4 cups (960 ml) no-salt-added vegetable stock

¼ cup + 2 tbsp (90 g) natural peanut butter

1 tbsp (17 g) white miso paste

2½ tbsp (25 g) curry powder

¼ tsp salt, or to taste

¼ tsp chili flakes

1 (14-oz [400-ml]) can full-fat coconut milk

1½ tbsp (22 ml) soy sauce

2 tsp (10 ml) sesame oil

1 (12-oz [350-g]) block extra firm tofu, diced

7 oz (194 g) buckwheat noodles

1 tbsp (15 ml) rice vinegar

2 tbsp (30 ml) lime juice, about 1 lime, plus more as desired

3 heads bok choy, sliced

SERVES 4

PREP: 5 MINUTES
COOK: 25 MINUTES
TOTAL: 30 MINUTES

1 yellow onion, finely diced

1 tbsp (15 ml) olive oil

1½ tsp (9 g) salt

4 cloves garlic, minced

¼ tsp pepper

½ tsp dried basil

½ tsp dried oregano

1 tsp Italian seasoning

1 (12-oz [350-g]) block extra firm tofu, crumbled

1 (28-oz [796-ml]) can crushed tomatoes

¼ cup (60 ml) plant-based milk (I used unsweetened oat milk)

4 cups (960 ml) no-salt-added vegetable stock

1 tbsp (13 g) granulated sugar

5 lasagna noodles, broken into bite-sized pieces

¼ cup (44 g) nutritional yeast

SIMPLE LASAGNA SOUP

My partner and I have a running joke that he is the expert when it comes to any recipe that's tomato-based, and lasagna is no exception. He makes the absolute best vegan lasagna that I swear gets more and more delicious every time he makes it. With that being said, there's no question that lasagna takes a significant amount of time and effort to make. Cue this Simple Lasagna Soup. It comes together in 30 minutes and has all the delicious flavors of lasagna, without all of the time required to make it. The crushed tomato base of the soup pairs perfectly with the Italian seasoning, while the crumbled tofu acts like a vegan meat and the lasagna noodles make it even more hearty and filling. I've added nutritional yeast for a cheesy flavor, but feel free to top it with shredded vegan cheese, too! Of course, I got his approval on this recipe, so you know it's going to be delicious!

1. In a large pot over medium heat, sauté the onion with the olive oil and salt until the onion is translucent, 3 to 4 minutes.

2. Add the garlic, pepper, basil, oregano and Italian seasoning, and sauté for another 2 to 3 minutes, until the garlic is lightly golden brown, being careful not to burn it.

3. Add the tofu, tomatoes, plant-based milk, vegetable stock and sugar. Stir to combine. Increase the heat to medium-high to bring the soup to a low boil, then cover and reduce it back to low heat to let it simmer for 10 minutes.

4. After 10 minutes, add the broken lasagna noodles and cook them in the soup as per package instructions. Add the nutritional yeast.

5. Refrigerate leftovers in an airtight container for up to 4 days.

RECIPE NOTE: If storing leftovers, the lasagna noodles may absorb some of the soup liquid. I recommend storing the lasagna noodles separately to avoid this.

LEMON CHICKPEA ORZO SOUP

Some soups feel like a warm hug, and this is definitely one of them. This soup is a spinoff of a super popular recipe on my website, Chickpea Noodle Soup, but this version is more lemon forward and uses orzo rather than fusilli pasta. The result is a bright, warming soup that's well-balanced with plant-based protein from the chickpeas, energizing carbohydrates from the orzo and micronutrients and fiber from the vegetables. I love making this soup ahead of a busy week so I have something nourishing to eat for lunch or as a quick dinner option.

1. In a large pot over medium heat, sauté the onion, carrots and celery in olive oil until the onion is translucent, 3 to 4 minutes.

2. Add the garlic, oregano, salt and pepper, and sauté them for another 2 to 3 minutes, until the garlic is lightly golden brown, but not burnt.

3. Add the vegetable stock, tahini and chickpeas. Increase the heat to medium-high, bringing the soup to a low boil, then reduce the heat back down to low with the lid on, simmering for 15 minutes.

4. Meanwhile, in a separate pot, cook the orzo as per package instructions.

5. Add the lemon juice to the soup. Once the orzo has finished cooking, add ½ cup (100 g) of orzo to a bowl with one-quarter of the soup.

6. Refrigerate any leftover soup and orzo separately in airtight containers for up to 4 days.

RECIPE NOTE: I recommend cooking and adding the orzo individually to each bowl of soup, as the orzo will absorb a lot of the liquid if you're cooking it in the soup and storing them together as leftovers.

30-MINUTE MEAL

SERVES 4

PREP: 10 MINUTES
COOK: 20 MINUTES
TOTAL: 30 MINUTES

1 yellow onion, diced
2 large carrots, diced
3 stalks celery, diced
1 tbsp (15 ml) olive oil
3 cloves garlic, minced
2 tsp (2 g) dried oregano
1 tsp salt, or to taste
¼ tsp pepper, or to taste
6 cups (1.4 L) no-salt-added vegetable stock
1 tbsp (15 g) tahini
1 (19-oz [540-g]) can chickpeas, drained and rinsed
1 cup (200 g) dried orzo
¼ cup (60 ml) lemon juice, about 1 lemon

BALANCED
SALADS &
BOWLS

You might be surprised to know that even though I eat a plant-based diet, I'm *very* picky about my salads. I like to make sure that they hit all the necessary food groups, have a variety of textures and flavors and include a delicious dressing. Gone are the days of the boring salads comprised of limp lettuce and a flavorless dressing. These salads and bowls are well-balanced, meaning they provide a great source of protein, carbohydrates and fat, so you'll stay full for longer than five minutes. And most importantly, they actually taste good, too!

"Bowls" can vary a lot depending on who you talk to. To me, a "bowl" is usually a one-pan recipe that can be thrown together in, you guessed it, a bowl and topped with a delicious sauce to tie it all together. They're different from salads because they're usually comprised of cooked vegetables rather than raw, but they can have a little freshness in there, too. Okay, maybe there's some overlap between what qualifies as a salad and a bowl, but either way, they're both delicious options and are usually super nutritious. I love reaching for bowls when I'm craving something a little warmer and heartier than a salad but still want something packed with vegetables.

If you're looking for a super quick dinner recipe to throw together, I highly suggest making my Easy Lemon-Pepper Tofu Bowl (page 92) or Savory Brussels Sprouts & Tofu Bacon Bowl (page 83). For a fresh salad option that the whole family will love, try the Lemon-Tahini White Bean Caesar Salad (page 80) or the Best Ever Taco Salad (page 84)!

BASIL LENTIL PASTA SALAD

I love pasta salads because they're the perfect option to make ahead of a busy week and can be more filling than a traditional salad. This Basil Lentil Pasta Salad has quickly become a weekday lunch staple for me because of how quick and easy it is to throw together, plus there's minimal cooking required. The lemon, Italian-inspired dressing pairs perfectly with the fresh basil, bell pepper, red onion, cherry tomatoes and Kalamata olives, plus we add lentils for a healthy dose of protein and fiber. I recommend using canned lentils to help this recipe come together even more quickly! This is the perfect packable lunch recipe that keeps well in the fridge for several days.

1. Cook the pasta as per package instructions in salted pasta water.

2. Meanwhile, begin making the salad by adding the red onion, bell pepper, cherry tomatoes, basil, lentils and olives to a large bowl. In a separate bowl, whisk together the olive oil, lemon juice, garlic, olive juice, Italian seasoning, salt and pepper to make the dressing. Add the dressing to the salad bowl.

3. Once the pasta has finished cooking, add it to the bowl with the salad and toss well to combine everything.

4. Refrigerate leftovers in an airtight container for up to 5 days.

RECIPE NOTES: If you're eating this as leftovers, you may want to add an additional tablespoon of olive oil or lemon juice to add moisture.

I love using bowtie pasta in this recipe, but feel free to use any type of pasta you prefer.

SERVES 4

PREP: 10 MINUTES
COOK: 7 MINUTES
TOTAL: 17 MINUTES

FOR THE SALAD

14 oz (400 g) bowtie pasta (see Recipe Notes)

Salt, as needed

½ red onion, diced

1 orange bell pepper, diced

1 cup (150 g) cherry tomatoes, quartered

½ cup (12 g) basil, julienned

1 (19-oz [540-g]) can lentils, drained and rinsed

½ cup (90 g) Kalamata olives, finely chopped

FOR THE DRESSING

¼ cup (60 ml) olive oil

¼ cup (60 ml) lemon juice, about 1 lemon

1 clove garlic, minced

1 tbsp (15 ml) olive juice

1 tbsp (6 g) Italian seasoning

¼ tsp salt, or to taste

¼ tsp pepper, or to taste

SERVES 4

PREP: 5 MINUTES
INACTIVE: 30 MINUTES
COOK: 30 MINUTES
TOTAL: 1 HOUR
5 MINUTES

1 block (250 g) tempeh
3 tbsp (45 ml) olive oil, divided
3 tbsp (51 g) white miso paste
2 tbsp (30 ml) Dijon mustard
2 tbsp (30 ml) maple syrup
2 tbsp (30 ml) rice vinegar
½ tbsp (7 ml) soy sauce
1 yellow bell pepper, sliced
2 cups (182 g) broccoli florets
1 tsp garlic powder
¼ tsp salt

MISO-DIJON GLAZED TEMPEH BOWL

I've always enjoyed exploring new-to-me flavor combinations, and this Miso-Dijon Glazed Tempeh Bowl is no exception. If you've never had miso paste before, it's a fermented soybean paste that has a salty, savory, umami flavor. Miso paste is also a great source of probiotics, which help us maintain good gut health. There are lots of different types of miso paste, but I've used white miso paste in this recipe since it has the mildest flavor. While this recipe says it takes just over one hour to make, 30 minutes is inactive time when the tempeh is marinating, and another 20 minutes is spent cooking the ingredients in the oven. Feel free to eat this tempeh bowl with rice, quinoa or another grain to make it more filling.

1. Steam your tempeh in 1 inch (2.5 cm) of water for 8 to 10 minutes. Steaming the tempeh helps to remove the bitterness and helps the tempeh absorb the marinade better.

2. Cut your tempeh block in half widthwise, so you have two thinner rectangles of tempeh. Cut each of those rectangles into 16 triangles, leaving you with 32 triangles of tempeh.

3. In a large bowl, whisk together 2 tablespoons (30 ml) of olive oil, the miso paste, Dijon mustard, maple syrup, rice vinegar and soy sauce. Place the tempeh in the bowl, toss to coat, cover and let marinate for 30 minutes in the fridge.

4. Preheat your oven to 450°F (232°C) and line two baking sheets with parchment paper.

5. In a large bowl, toss together the bell pepper, broccoli, remaining tablespoon (15 ml) of olive oil, garlic powder and salt.

6. Once the tempeh has been marinated, place it on the baking sheet, spacing it out evenly. Reserve the remaining marinade. Spread the bell pepper and broccoli on a baking sheet, too, and put everything in the oven for 20 minutes, flipping halfway through, until the tempeh is golden brown on each side.

7. Add 1 to 2 tablespoons (15 to 30 ml) of water to the leftover marinade to drizzle on top of the tempeh and veggies once they're done cooking.

8. Refrigerate leftovers in an airtight container for up to 4 days.

EDAMAME CRUNCH SALAD WITH PEANUT DRESSING

Meals that require minimal cooking are my go-tos in the summer, since the last thing I want to do on a hot day is turn on the oven. Enter this Edamame Crunch Salad with Peanut Dressing. This perfectly crunchy, cold, protein-packed salad with a nutty, drool-worthy sauce will keep you energized throughout your day. Yes, it does require a bit of cooking for the quinoa and edamame, but it takes less than 15 minutes and won't heat up your entire home. One of the best parts about this salad, other than it coming together in less than 30 minutes, is that it stores as leftovers really well, making it the perfect quick and easy meal prep option.

1. Cook the quinoa as per the package instructions. Steam the edamame according to the package instructions. Allow the quinoa and edamame to cool while you prepare the rest of the ingredients.

2. Once the quinoa and edamame are cooked and have cooled, combine them with the red cabbage, kale, carrot and sunflower seeds.

3. To make the peanut dressing, whisk together the peanut butter, rice vinegar, soy sauce, sesame oil, garlic powder, ginger powder, sriracha, lime juice, sugar and water, adding the water or plant-based milk as needed to reach your desired consistency. Add the dressing to the salad. You may not need to use all of the dressing. Toss well to combine everything.

4. If you don't plan on eating all of the salad at once, refrigerate the salad and dressing separately in airtight containers for up to 3 days.

RECIPE NOTES: It's important to make sure you're using shelled edamame for this recipe, otherwise you will have to remove the beans from the pods.

The amount of water or plant-based milk you'll need to thin the salad dressing will depend on how thick your peanut butter is. I used approximately 2 tablespoons (30 ml).

GOOD SOURCE OF PROTEIN, 30-MINUTE MEAL

SERVES 2

PREP: 10 MINUTES
COOK: 15 MINUTES
TOTAL: 25 MINUTES

FOR THE SALAD

½ cup (93 g) dried quinoa

2 cups (310 g) shelled edamame, fresh or frozen (see Recipe Notes)

2 cups (178 g) thinly sliced red cabbage

2 cups (134 g) packed kale, thinly sliced

1 carrot, grated

¼ cup (33 g) shelled sunflower seeds or pumpkin seeds

FOR THE PEANUT DRESSING

½ cup (120 g) natural peanut butter

1½ tbsp (22 ml) rice vinegar

¾ tbsp (11 ml) soy sauce

1½ tbsp (22 ml) sesame oil

¾ tsp garlic powder

¾ tsp ginger powder

1½ tsp (7 ml) sriracha

3 tbsp (45 ml) lime juice, about 1½ limes

¾ tbsp granulated sugar or maple syrup

2–3 tbsp (30–45 ml) water or plant-based milk to thin, as needed (I used unsweetened oat milk; see Recipe Notes)

SERVES 2

PREP: 20 MINUTES
TOTAL TIME: 20 MINUTES

FOR THE DRESSING
¼ cup (60 g) tahini

1 tbsp (15 ml) olive oil

¼ cup (60 ml) lemon juice,
about 1 lemon

1 tbsp (15 ml) Dijon mustard

1 clove garlic

2 tbsp (22 g) nutritional yeast

1 tbsp (15 ml) maple syrup or
other sweetener

½ tsp salt, or to taste

¼ tsp pepper, or to taste

3 tbsp (45 ml) water, plus
more as needed

FOR THE VEGAN PARMESAN
⅓ cup (44 g) raw, hulled,
unsalted sunflower seeds

½ tsp salt

2 tbsp (22 g) nutritional yeast

FOR THE SALAD
4 cups (268 g) kale, diced

1 tsp apple cider vinegar

¼ red onion, sliced

1 (19-oz [540-g]) can white
beans, drained and rinsed

OPTIONAL TOPPINGS
Additional vegan Parmesan

Cracked black pepper

Fresh lemon juice

LEMON-TAHINI WHITE BEAN CAESAR SALAD

Growing up, I was a pretty picky eater. The only vegetables I liked were raw baby carrots (yes, they had to be raw) and plain romaine lettuce. I have vivid memories of asking my mom if I could snack on the plain romaine lettuce she was chopping while making a salad. As I got a few years older, my palate expanded only slightly and I started to enjoy Caesar salads. I'm happy to say that now I enjoy a wide variety of foods, but once I went plant-based, I was nervous that I'd never be able to have a good Caesar salad again. Luckily that hasn't been a problem, especially with this recipe. The keys to a good plant-based Caesar salad in my book are a garlicky, creamy, lemon dressing paired with fresh lettuce or kale and a delicious, salty vegan Parmesan. While this salad definitely isn't a classic Caesar, it's still wildly delicious and one that I think my younger self would be proud of.

1. In a high-speed blender, blend the tahini, olive oil, lemon juice, Dijon mustard, garlic, nutritional yeast, maple syrup, salt, pepper and water to make the dressing. Add more water to adjust the consistency to your liking.

2. Using a small food processor, coffee grinder or blender, blend the sunflower seeds, salt and nutritional yeast until the vegan Parmesan has the texture of sand.

3. In a large bowl, sprinkle the kale with apple cider vinegar. Using your hands, massage the kale and apple cider vinegar together until the kale is slightly wilted and darker green, 2 to 3 minutes.

4. Add the onion, white beans, 2 tablespoons (30 g) of the vegan Parmesan and the salad dressing to the kale. Toss well to combine everything. Feel free to serve it with additional vegan Parmesan, pepper and lemon juice.

5. Refrigerate salad leftovers in an airtight container for up to 3 days. Refrigerate leftover vegan Parmesan separately in an airtight container for up to 2 weeks.

RECIPE NOTES: You can definitely use romaine lettuce in this recipe if you'd prefer it over kale!

You'll likely have leftover vegan Parmesan. Feel free to use it in pastas, salads and even on popcorn!

SAVORY BRUSSELS SPROUTS & TOFU BACON BOWL

GOOD SOURCE OF PROTEIN, ONE-POT MEAL

If you were to ask me what my favorite vegetable is, I'd probably say Brussels sprouts. I love that they have a delicious, charred flavor when roasted properly and how well they hold up in salads. This Savory Brussels Sprouts & Tofu Bacon Bowl is a spin on the classic dish of Brussels sprouts and bacon, but I added potatoes to make it a little more filling. While the tofu crumble bacon obviously doesn't taste exactly like bacon, I think it does a great job of adding a salty, smoky, slightly sweet flavor that's similar to regular bacon. To make things even more delicious, I've added a tahini sauce that is not only amazing on this bowl, but on pretty much everything else, too.

SERVES 4

PREP: 15 MINUTES
COOK: 25–30 MINUTES
TOTAL: 40–45 MINUTES

1. Preheat the oven to 450°F (232°C). Line two baking sheets with parchment paper.

2. Combine the Brussels sprouts, potatoes, olive oil, garlic powder, onion powder, paprika, oregano and salt in a large bowl and toss well to combine everything. Spread the mixture evenly on a baking sheet and bake for 25 to 30 minutes, until the potatoes are golden brown and fork tender, flipping halfway through.

3. Meanwhile, combine the tofu, olive oil, maple syrup, smoked paprika, garlic powder, soy sauce and liquid smoke in a large bowl and toss well to combine everything. Spread the mixture evenly on a baking sheet, and place it in the oven along with the potatoes and Brussels sprouts after they've been cooking for 10 minutes.

4. Bake the tofu bacon for 15 to 20 minutes, until it has dried out slightly and is golden brown, flipping halfway through.

5. For the sauce, whisk or blend together the tahini, nutritional yeast, garlic, soy sauce, water, lemon juice and maple syrup.

6. Once all the components are done, add the Brussels sprouts, potatoes, and tofu bacon to a bowl and top with the sauce to serve.

7. Refrigerate leftovers separately in airtight containers for up to 4 days.

RECIPE NOTE: Make sure to dice the potatoes small enough so they cook evenly with the Brussels sprouts.

FOR THE BRUSSELS SPROUTS & POTATOES

4 cups (352 g) Brussels sprouts, quartered

3 medium yellow potatoes, diced into 1-inch (2.5-cm) cubes (see Recipe Note)

1½ tbsp (22 ml) olive oil

1 tsp garlic powder

1 tsp onion powder

1 tsp smoked paprika

1 tsp oregano

½ tsp salt

FOR THE TOFU

1 (12-oz [350-g]) block extra firm tofu, crumbled

2 tsp (10 ml) olive oil

2 tbsp (30 ml) maple syrup

3 tsp (9 g) smoked paprika

2 tsp garlic powder

2 tbsp (30 ml) soy sauce

2 tsp (10 ml) liquid smoke

FOR THE SAUCE

⅓ cup (80 g) tahini

3 tbsp (33 g) nutritional yeast

1 clove garlic, minced

1 tbsp (15 ml) soy sauce

½ cup (120 ml) water

2 tbsp (30 ml) lemon juice, about ½ lemon

1 tbsp (15 ml) maple syrup

BEST EVER TACO SALAD

When I want something quick and easy with minimal effort, taco salads tend to be at the top of my list. They're simple and nourishing but still so satisfying. Plus, you can completely customize them based on your taste preferences. The star of the show for this taco salad is the spiced black beans, which take 15 minutes or less to make but add so much flavor. Black beans are also a great source of iron, fiber and plant-based protein to help us feel fuller and more energized for longer. While this taco salad definitely isn't authentic, it has a lot of the fresh flavors of Mexican-inspired food and is super delicious.

SERVES 4

PREP: 15 MINUTES
COOK: 15 MINUTES
TOTAL: 30 MINUTES

1 cup (200 g) uncooked brown rice
2 small sweet potatoes, diced

FOR THE BEANS
2 (19-oz [540-g]) cans black beans, drained and rinsed
1½ tbsp (22 ml) olive oil
2 tsp (6 g) chili powder
1 tsp garlic powder
1 tsp smoked paprika
½ tsp chili flakes, plus more as desired
½ tsp liquid smoke, optional
¼ tsp pepper
½ tsp salt

FOR THE MAYO
½ cup (120 ml) vegan mayonnaise
3 tbsp (45 ml) lime juice, about 1½ limes
1 tbsp (15 ml) sriracha, plus more as desired

FOR ASSEMBLY
8 cups (376 g) romaine, diced
2 yellow bell peppers, diced
2 Roma tomatoes, diced
1 green onion, sliced
1⅓ cups (345 g) salsa
2 cups (52 g) corn chips, crumbled
½ cup (8 g) fresh cilantro, roughly chopped
Lime juice, to taste

1. Cook the rice as per package instructions. Steam the sweet potatoes until they're fork tender.

2. Meanwhile, in a large pan over medium heat, sauté the black beans in olive oil with the chili powder, garlic powder, smoked paprika, chili flakes, liquid smoke, if using, pepper and salt for 10 to 15 minutes, until the beans start to crack open.

3. Whisk together the vegan mayonnaise, lime juice and sriracha for the sriracha mayo. Set this aside.

4. To serve, add to each bowl 2 cups (94 g) of romaine, ½ diced bell pepper, ½ diced tomato, ¼ sliced green onion, ⅓ cup (86 g) of salsa, ½ diced sweet potato, ½ cup (101 g) of brown rice, ½ cup (13 g) of crumbled corn chips, 1 cup (135 g) of spiced black beans, 2 tablespoons (2 g) of fresh cilantro and sriracha mayo to taste. Mix everything together and enjoy with additional lime juice, to taste.

5. Refrigerate leftovers separately in airtight containers for up to 4 days.

RECIPE NOTES: The smaller you dice the sweet potatoes, the faster they'll steam. I recommend dicing into 1-inch (2.5-cm) cubes.

Feel free to change up the toppings based on your taste preferences.

CABBAGE, CUCUMBER & PUMPKIN SEED SALAD WITH GREEN GODDESS DRESSING

GOOD SOURCE
OF FIBER,
15-MINUTE MEAL

SERVES 2

PREP: 15 MINUTES
TOTAL: 15 MINUTES

If you think salads are boring, this one is for you. It uses cabbage, grated carrot and pumpkin seeds as a crunchy base, plus lentils for plant-based protein and a mouth-watering, fresh basil salad dressing that I promise will have you craving this salad nonstop. This salad was inspired by the Baked by Melissa Green Goddess Salad. I wanted to put my own spin on the recipe by adding some more plant-based protein from the lentils and adjusting the dressing a bit based on my own taste preferences. This salad requires absolutely no cooking if you're using canned lentils. If you want it to come together even faster than it already does, I recommend using store-bought pre-chopped cabbage slaw rather than chopping your own.

1. For the dressing, add the olive oil, basil, spinach, garlic, lemon juice, apple cider vinegar, nutritional yeast, salt and sunflower seeds to a high-speed blender and blend until it's smooth.

2. To create the salad, in a large bowl, combine the cabbage, grated carrot, lentils, cucumber and pumpkin seeds together. Pour the dressing over the top and toss it well.

3. Refrigerate any leftovers in an airtight container for up to 3 days.

FOR THE DRESSING

3 tbsp (45 ml) olive oil

½ cup (12 g) fresh basil leaves, packed

1 cup (30 g) spinach, packed

2 cloves garlic

¼ cup (60 ml) lemon juice, about 1 lemon

1 tbsp (15 ml) apple cider vinegar

3 tbsp (33 g) nutritional yeast

½ tsp salt

¼ cup (33 g) sunflower seeds, cashews or pumpkin seeds

FOR THE SALAD

3 cups (267 g) sliced purple cabbage, about ½ cabbage

1 carrot, grated

1 (19-oz [540-g]) can lentils, drained and rinsed

½ cucumber, finely diced

⅓ cup (45 g) shelled pumpkin seeds

LEMON, LENTIL & QUINOA SALAD

This Lemon, Lentil & Quinoa Salad was one of the first recipes that I tested for this cookbook, and I immediately knew I had to include it. I love that this salad can be whipped up super quickly if you have guests over unexpectedly or need a side ASAP, and it's more filling than the average leafy side salad because of the lentils and quinoa. It also uses ingredients that you probably already have on hand and is a great option to make in larger batches to rely on throughout the week or to bring to barbecues and potlucks. I originally created this salad to pair with veggie burgers, sandwiches or soups, but feel free to eat it with whatever you'd like or eat a larger portion as a main!

FOR THE SALAD

1 cup (186 g) uncooked quinoa

2 cups (480 ml) no-salt-added vegetable stock, for cooking the quinoa

1 (19-oz [540-g]) can lentils, drained and rinsed

½ yellow bell pepper

½ cucumber, quartered and sliced

1 cup (89 g) sliced cabbage

FOR THE DRESSING

3 tbsp (45 ml) olive oil

¼ cup (60 ml) lemon juice, about 1 lemon

2 cloves garlic, minced

1½ tbsp (22 ml) Dijon mustard

1½ tbsp (22 ml) apple cider vinegar

½ tsp oregano

½ tsp salt

½ tsp pepper

1. Cook the quinoa as per package instructions, using vegetable stock instead of water.

2. In a large bowl, begin making the salad by combining the lentils, bell pepper, cucumber, cabbage and cooked quinoa. In a small bowl, whisk together the olive oil, lemon juice, garlic, Dijon mustard, apple cider vinegar, oregano, salt and pepper for the dressing. Add the salad dressing to the salad.

3. Refrigerate any leftovers in an airtight container for up to 5 days.

BEET & QUINOA SALAD WITH MAPLE VINAIGRETTE

One of my favorite tips to give clients is to try to eat at least 30 different plant-based foods throughout the week. This is not only beneficial for making sure we're getting a wide variety of nutrients, but also helps to maintain a diversity of gut bacteria, and good gut health in general. Thirty different foods may sound like a lot, but I'd bet within one day you get at least 10 to 15 different foods, since spices and herbs totally count! For me, one of the ways I try to introduce variety is by grabbing a different vegetable or fruit each week that isn't in my typical grocery shop! When I was developing this recipe, beets were my "different" vegetable. While I've had them plenty of times, they aren't part of my weekly rotation. I love the subtle earthiness of beets and how well they pair with this sweet maple vinaigrette and peppery arugula in this salad. This recipe stores well in the fridge, so it's a great prep-ahead option!

1. Preheat the oven to 425°F (218°C). Line a baking sheet with parchment paper.

2. In a medium bowl, toss the beet pieces in olive oil and spread them on the baking sheet. Roast them for 25 to 30 minutes, or until fork tender. Meanwhile, cook the quinoa in the vegetable stock as per package instructions.

3. Once the beet pieces are cooked, combine them with the quinoa, arugula, walnuts, apple, salt and pepper together in a large bowl.

4. In a separate bowl, whisk the maple syrup, lemon juice, olive oil, garlic, Dijon mustard, salt and pepper together for the maple vinaigrette. Toss the salad with the maple vinaigrette.

5. Refrigerate any leftovers in an airtight container for up to 3 days.

> RECIPE NOTE: I didn't bother peeling the beet in this recipe—I just washed it really well. If you choose to peel your beet, I recommend you do this under cool running water and make sure you're wearing an apron!

GOOD SOURCE OF IRON AND OMEGA-3

SERVES 2

PREP: 5 MINUTES
COOK: 30 MINUTES
TOTAL: 35 MINUTES

FOR THE SALAD

1 beet, diced (see Recipe Note)

1 tbsp (15 ml) olive oil

1 cup (186 g) uncooked quinoa

2 cups (480 ml) no-salt-added vegetable stock

4 cups (80 g) arugula, packed

⅔ cup (67 g) walnut halves

1 apple, diced (I used Pink Lady)

Salt and pepper, to taste

FOR THE VINAIGRETTE

2 tbsp (30 ml) maple syrup

¼ cup (60 ml) lemon juice, about 1 lemon

3 tbsp (45 ml) olive oil

1 clove garlic, minced

1 tbsp (15 ml) Dijon mustard

¼ tsp salt

¼ tsp pepper

SERVES 3

PREP: 10 MINUTES
COOK: 25 MINUTES
TOTAL: 35 MINUTES

FOR SERVING

1½ cups (303 g) cooked brown rice, quinoa, couscous or other grain

FOR THE TOFU & GREEN BEANS

1 (12-oz [350-g]) block extra firm tofu, diced

13 oz (365 g) green beans, with the ends trimmed off

1 tbsp (15 ml) olive oil

3 tsp (9 g) lemon pepper seasoning

3 cloves garlic, minced

½ tsp salt

FOR THE HUMMUS SAUCE

¼ cup (63 g) garlic or plain hummus

2 tbsp (30 ml) lemon juice, about ½ lemon

½ tsp lemon pepper seasoning, or to taste

EASY LEMON-PEPPER TOFU BOWL

Whenever I'm looking for a super quick, easy meal, I usually turn to some sort of bowl. I try to make sure my bowl recipes have a good source of plant-based protein, fiber-rich carbohydrates, healthy fat, veggies and, obviously, they have to taste amazing. This Easy Lemon-Pepper Tofu Bowl definitely checks all of the boxes. We use my favorite hack for making a quick and easy sauce: whisking together hummus and lemon juice! This recipe uses pre-cooked brown rice, quinoa or couscous to make it come together more quickly. I recommend cooking one of these grains during your weekly meal prep! If you don't have anything prepped, try using couscous, as it only takes 5 minutes to cook.

1. Preheat the oven to 450°F (232°C). Line a baking sheet with parchment paper.

2. In a large bowl, toss together the tofu, green beans, olive oil, lemon pepper seasoning, garlic and salt. Spread the mixture evenly on the baking sheet, and bake for 25 minutes, or until the tofu is lightly golden brown, flipping halfway through.

3. Meanwhile, in a small bowl, whisk together the hummus, lemon juice and lemon pepper seasoning for the hummus sauce. Set it aside.

4. Once the tofu and green beans have finished cooking, combine them in a bowl with your cooked grain of choice and a drizzle of the hummus sauce.

5. Refrigerate leftovers separately in airtight containers for up to 4 days.

CREAMY DILL PICKLE SALAD

I was inspired to make this Creamy Dill Pickle Salad after a recent trip to Costco where I saw that they had dill pickle salad kits. I know what you might be thinking . . . dill pickle salad? But something about it sounded super delicious to me, so I had to try my own spin on it. I can definitely confirm that this salad is unexpectedly amazing. It's the perfect mix of salty, garlicky and crunchy. We use roasted chickpeas for a delicious plant-based protein that also provides a crunch, plus plenty of veggies like kale, cabbage and celery and, of course, a creamy dill pickle dressing that ties it all together. Don't knock it 'til you try it!

1. Preheat the oven to 450°F (232°C) and line a baking sheet with parchment paper.

2. To make the roasted chickpeas, combine the chickpeas, olive oil, garlic powder, onion powder, salt and pepper in a large bowl and toss everything well. Spread the mixture evenly on the baking sheet, making sure to leave enough space between the chickpeas, and bake for 20 to 25 minutes, until they're golden brown and crispy, flipping halfway through.

3. Meanwhile, add the sunflower seeds, lemon juice, dill, pickles, pickle juice, garlic, nutritional yeast, onion powder, maple syrup and water to a high-speed blender and blend the dressing until it's smooth.

4. To assemble the salad, add the kale, cabbage, celery and pickles into a large bowl. Add the roasted chickpeas and 1¼ cups (300 ml) of the dill dressing, and toss well to combine. Feel free to add additional dressing if needed.

5. Refrigerate leftovers in an airtight container for up to 3 days.

> RECIPE NOTES: Depending on your blender, you may need more or less water for the dill dressing.
>
> You may have about ½ cup (120 ml) of dressing left over, depending on how dressed you like your salad. Feel free to use this as a dipping sauce for veggies, fries or as a prepped salad dressing.

GOOD SOURCE OF PROTEIN

SERVES 2

PREP: 10 MINUTES
COOK: 25 MINUTES
TOTAL: 35 MINUTES

FOR THE ROASTED CHICKPEAS

1 (19-oz [540-g]) can chickpeas, drained and rinsed

1 tbsp (15 ml) olive oil

1 tsp garlic powder

1 tsp onion powder

½ tsp salt

¼ tsp pepper

FOR THE DILL DRESSING

½ cup (67 g) raw, hulled, unsalted sunflower seeds

¼ cup (60 ml) lemon juice, about 1 lemon

2 tbsp (1 g) fresh dill

2 medium-sized dill pickles

½ cup (120 ml) pickle juice

1 clove garlic

3 tbsp (33 g) nutritional yeast

1 tsp onion powder

1 tbsp (15 ml) maple syrup

¼–½ cup (60–120 ml) water, plus more as needed

FOR ASSEMBLY

1½ cups (101 g) julienned kale

1½ cups (134 g) sliced cabbage

2 stalks celery, diced

3 medium-sized dill pickles, diced

SIMPLE
SIDES

Even before I was plant-based, I was always that person at holiday dinners who cared way more about the side dishes than the main. I mean, how could you go wrong with stuffing, mashed potatoes and roasted veggies? Even today, some of my favorite recipes are technically side dishes, like my Basil Pesto Potatoes (page 110) or Curry Sweet Potato Fries with Maple-Dijon Dipping Sauce (page 101).

These simple side dishes are a great addition when you need a little *more* with your meal, or they're a creative way to add some extra veggies! If you're not a huge fan of vegetables, I recommend switching up the way that you cook them by using some of these recipes! I also recommend switching up the types of vegetables you eat, as well as how they're prepared. Chances are there are plenty of vegetables out there that you've never tried. Personally, I only really liked raw vegetables before going plant-based, but now I can't get enough of my Garlic-Roasted Green Beans (page 109) or Maple-Roasted Carrots (page 98)!

MAPLE-ROASTED CARROTS

Side dishes can often be an afterthought, but not these Maple-Roasted Carrots. I promise you that these will be the star of whatever meal you're cooking. They have a delicious sweet-and-savory flavor from the garlic, coriander and maple syrup, and they're totally kid-approved! Plus, they're pretty hands off, since you can toss all of the ingredients together and throw them in the oven, leaving you more time to work on the main dish!

5 medium carrots, cut into batons (thick sticks)

1 tbsp (15 ml) melted coconut oil (see Recipe Notes)

1 tbsp + 2 tsp (25 ml) maple syrup, divided

1 tsp garlic powder

2 cloves garlic, minced

½ tsp ground coriander

½ tsp salt, divided

¼ tsp pepper

1. Preheat the oven to 450°F (232°C) and line a baking sheet with parchment paper.

2. In a large bowl, combine the carrots, coconut oil, 1 tablespoon (15 ml) of maple syrup, garlic powder, garlic, coriander, ¼ teaspoon of salt and pepper.

3. Lay the carrots on the baking sheet, ensuring there's enough space between the carrots. Bake them for 20 to 25 minutes, until the carrots are fork tender, flipping once halfway through.

4. Remove the carrots from the oven, and top them with the remaining 2 teaspoons (10 ml) of maple syrup and ¼ teaspoon of salt. Stir well to combine.

RECIPE NOTES: The coconut oil adds a great flavor to the carrots, but if you don't like coconut or don't have it on hand, feel free to substitute with a neutral tasting oil, like avocado oil.

Make sure the carrots are well spaced out when roasting them. If there isn't enough room between the carrots, they'll steam rather than roast. This goes for anything you're roasting!

CURRY SWEET POTATO FRIES WITH MAPLE-DIJON DIPPING SAUCE

ONE-POT MEAL

SERVES 2

PREP: 5 MINUTES
COOK: 25–30 MINUTES
TOTAL: 30–35 MINUTES

These Curry Sweet Potato Fries with Maple-Dijon Dipping Sauce are the perfect side dish to pair with any sandwich or veggie burger! I know there are a lot of questions about how to make delicious baked "fries," so here are some of my tips. First, make sure you're cooking at a high enough temperature to get that crispy outer layer. I also recommend ensuring you're leaving enough space between the fries so that they roast, rather than steam. This is my number one tip for any food you're roasting! Lastly, use some oil, as the recipe calls for, to help them roast. The trick is to use *some* oil, but not *too much,* so that they stay moist but not greasy. It's also important to remember that it's super hard to replicate a *true* french fry without actually frying. If you have an air fryer, this is a great recipe to use it!

FOR THE FRIES

2 medium sweet potatoes, cut into fries

1 tbsp (15 ml) olive oil

1 tsp garlic powder

1 tsp curry powder

½ tsp salt

FOR THE DIPPING SAUCE

2 tbsp (30 ml) Dijon mustard

1 tbsp (15 ml) maple syrup

1. Preheat the oven to 450°F (232°C). Line a baking sheet with parchment paper.

2. In a large bowl, toss together the sweet potatoes, olive oil, garlic powder, curry powder and salt. Spread the mixture evenly on the baking sheet, leaving enough room between the fries.

3. Bake them for 25 to 30 minutes, or until the sweet potatoes are lightly golden brown and crispy, flipping halfway through.

4. Meanwhile, whisk together the Dijon mustard and maple syrup for the dipping sauce.

5. Refrigerate leftover sweet potato fries and dipping sauce in separate airtight containers for up to 4 days.

RECIPE NOTES: To cook these in an air fryer, cook at 400°F (204°C) for 20 to 25 minutes, shaking or flipping halfway through, or until lightly golden brown and crispy.

I left the skin on these sweet potato fries for extra nutrients, but feel free to peel them if you prefer.

SERVES 4

PREP: 5 MINUTES
COOK: 20–25 MINUTES
TOTAL: 25–30 MINUTES

1 large head of cauliflower, cut
into florets
1 tbsp (15 ml) olive oil
1 tsp smoked paprika
1 tsp garlic powder
½ tsp salt
¼ tsp pepper

SMOKY ROASTED CAULIFLOWER

Would it be super predictable and dietitian-y of me if I said that roasted cauliflower might be one of my favorite foods ever? I just love how versatile roasted cauliflower can be and how the crispiness adds so much flavor. A lot of people think cauliflower isn't very nutritious since it's not a colorful vegetable, but even white vegetables contain nutrients like vitamin C, potassium and vitamin B6. Plus, cauliflower is a cruciferous vegetable, which means it contains a nutrient called sulforaphane that's been shown to help reduce the risk of developing certain types of cancer. If you want to know where to start with incorporating cauliflower into your regular eating pattern, this smoky roasted cauliflower is the perfect option!

1. Preheat the oven to 450°F (232°C) and line a baking sheet with parchment paper.

2. Combine the cauliflower, olive oil, smoked paprika, garlic powder, salt and pepper in a large bowl. Toss everything well to combine.

3. Spread the cauliflower evenly on the baking sheet. Roast it for 20 to 25 minutes, or until the cauliflower is fork tender and golden brown on the ends.

4. Refrigerate leftovers in an airtight container for up to 4 days.

RECIPE NOTE: To make this in the air fryer, I recommend cooking at 400°F (204°C) for 15 to 20 minutes, or until the cauliflower florets are fork tender and golden brown on the ends.

FRESH SESAME CUCUMBER SALAD

Sometimes I'm craving something salty and savory, but also want it to be light and nourishing. This Fresh Sesame Cucumber Salad is perfect for those times. It takes just a few minutes to throw together, and the sesame oil, chili flakes, rice vinegar and soy sauce pair perfectly together. I love having this cucumber salad as a side dish with a sandwich, curry or just on its own as a light snack.

1. Add the cucumber and salt to a medium bowl and toss them well to combine. Let it sit for 5 minutes, then with clean hands, squeeze out and drain off the excess water from the cucumbers.

2. Add the soy sauce, sesame oil, rice vinegar and chili flakes to the cucumber and stir to combine.

3. This is best eaten fresh, but leftovers can be refrigerated in an airtight container for up to 2 days.

RECIPE NOTE: The key to this recipe is slicing the cucumber super thin so it soaks up as much flavor as possible. I used a vegetable peeler to (carefully!) do this, but a mandolin would also work well.

10-MINUTE MEAL

SERVES 2

PREP: 5 MINUTES
INACTIVE: 5 MINUTES
TOTAL: 10 MINUTES

1 large cucumber, very thinly sliced (see Recipe Note)

⅛ tsp salt

2 tsp (10 ml) soy sauce

2 tsp (10 ml) sesame oil

2 tsp (10 ml) rice vinegar

¼ tsp chili flakes

PAN-FRIED BALSAMIC BROCCOLI & WALNUTS

1 tbsp (15 ml) olive oil

1 head of broccoli, cut into florets

½ tsp garlic powder

¼ tsp salt

1 tbsp (15 ml) balsamic vinegar

¼ cup (25 g) walnut pieces

I often get asked where I get my ideas for recipes, and my answer is "everywhere." I might have memories of a recipe with meat or dairy in it that I want to try, or I see recipe inspiration on Pinterest, or sometimes an idea just comes to me out of nowhere. That's what happened with this Pan-Fried Balsamic Broccoli & Walnuts. I knew I wanted to share a broccoli recipe that didn't require roasting, but I wanted it to be more interesting than just pan-fried broccoli. As I was cooking the recipe, I decided to add some walnuts and a splash of balsamic vinegar, and the result is one of my favorite side dish recipes I've ever created. It's so delicious that my partner and I ate the entire pan in less than five minutes. It's the perfect vegetable-heavy side dish when you want something quick and easy but that doesn't necessarily taste like you're just eating vegetables. I hope you love this one as much as I do!

1. Heat the olive oil in a large pan over medium heat. Add the broccoli florets to the pan and sprinkle them with garlic powder and salt. Sauté for 7 to 10 minutes, only mixing every 3 to 4 minutes so that the broccoli has a chance to lightly char.

2. Once the broccoli is lightly charred, add the balsamic vinegar and walnut pieces, and continue to sauté for another 2 to 3 minutes, being careful not to burn the walnuts.

3. This dish is best served fresh but can be refrigerated for up to 3 days in an airtight container.

RECIPE NOTES: Nuts can burn very quickly on the stove, so keep an eye on them while cooking.

I like to cook this recipe in my cast-iron pan since it adds some extra crispiness, but use whatever pan you have!

GARLIC-ROASTED GREEN BEANS

ONE-POT MEAL,
30-MINUTE MEAL

SERVES 2

PREP: 5 MINUTES
COOK: 25 MINUTES
TOTAL: 30 MINUTES

These Garlic-Roasted Green Beans are a easy one-pan side that pairs well with my One-Pan Mushroom Gnocchi (page 50) or Herby Lentil "Meatballs" & Garlic Bread (page 42). They're super flavorful from the garlic, nutritional yeast and lemon juice and can even be made in the air fryer. They're a super easy way to add greens to a meal that might be lacking in the veggie department. Fair warning that when I was testing this recipe, my partner and I almost ate the whole batch right from the pan, so you may want to double the recipe!

14 oz (394 g) green beans, ends removed

2 tbsp (30 ml) olive oil

3 cloves garlic, minced

½ tsp garlic powder

½ tsp salt, plus ⅛ tsp for topping

1 tbsp (11 g) nutritional yeast

2 tbsp (30 ml) lemon juice, about ½ lemon

1. Preheat the oven to 450°F (232°C) and line a baking sheet with parchment paper.

2. In a large bowl, toss the green beans with olive oil, garlic, garlic powder and ½ teaspoon of salt.

3. Spread the green beans evenly on the baking sheet and roast for 20 to 25 minutes, or until the beans are starting to crisp up and turn a light golden brown, flipping halfway through.

4. Remove the green beans from the oven and toss them in the same bowl used before with the remaining ⅛ teaspoon of salt, nutritional yeast and lemon juice.

5. Refrigerate leftovers in an airtight container for up to 4 days

RECIPE NOTES: If you're cooking these in the air fryer, cook them at 400°F (204°C) for 15 to 20 minutes, or until the green beans are golden brown and slightly crispy.

These are best served fresh, as they tend to lose their crispness when stored in the fridge.

FOR THE POTATOES

1½ lb (680 g) baby potatoes, sliced in half

1 tbsp (15 ml) olive oil

2 cloves garlic, minced

⅓ tsp salt

¼ tsp pepper

FOR THE PESTO

1 oz (28 g) fresh basil leaves

2 tbsp (30 ml) lemon juice, about ½ lemon

¼ cup (30 g) pumpkin seeds

1 clove garlic, minced

4 tbsp (60 ml) olive oil

2 tbsp (22 g) nutritional yeast

½ tsp salt

1 tbsp (15 ml) water to thin, or as needed

BASIL PESTO POTATOES

Sometimes I'll go months without craving a certain food or ingredient, then eat it again and become obsessed with it. That's how I feel about pesto. I love how flavorful pesto is, but so fresh and simple to make. You might not think that pesto and potatoes would pair so well together, but the bright and garlicky flavor of the pesto pairs perfectly with potatoes, which tend to be a bit heavier. Most pesto recipes use Parmesan cheese, so I've used nutritional yeast in place of that. I've also swapped out the typical pine nuts for pumpkin seeds since they're more cost-effective, but sunflower seeds would also work great!

1. Preheat the oven to 450°F (232°C) and line a baking sheet with parchment paper.

2. To prepare the potatoes, in a large bowl, toss the potatoes, olive oil, garlic, salt and pepper together. Spread the mixture evenly on the baking sheet so they're well spaced apart.

3. Roast them for 25 to 30 minutes, or until fork tender, flipping halfway through.

4. Meanwhile, add the basil, lemon juice, pumpkin seeds, garlic, olive oil, nutritional yeast, salt and water to a blender or food processor. Blend until the pesto is almost smooth and set aside.

5. Once the potatoes are done cooking, remove them from the pan and place them in the large bowl. Toss with the pesto, adding one spoonful of pesto at a time until you have the desired amount.

6. Refrigerate leftovers in an airtight container for up to 3 days.

RECIPE NOTES: I've used baby potatoes for this recipe, but yellow potatoes would also work well—just make sure to cut them small enough so that they cook quickly.

This recipe makes about ½ cup (100 g) of pesto. You may not use it all. I added a spoonful of pesto to the potatoes at a time until I was at my desired amount.

You may need additional water or olive oil to thin the pesto depending on your blender or food processor.

NOURISHING
BREAKFASTS
& SNACKS
ON THE GO

You've heard it before—breakfast is the most important meal of the day. While I actually think all meals are super important, starting our day off with a good balance of protein, carbs, fat, fiber and flavor helps to keep our blood sugar and energy levels balanced throughout the day. I've made sure that these breakfast recipes include all of these components so you can feel your best! For example, you'll find that My Everyday Ultimate Green Smoothie (page 123) uses soy milk for protein, peanut butter and flax seeds for healthy fats and a banana and strawberries for fiber and carbohydrates.

What's equally as important to me is that you're maintaining that fuel throughout the day by eating nourishing snacks. If you're hungry between meals, the best thing that you can do is eat! I recommend choosing snacks that have at least two of the following to help keep blood sugar and energy levels stable: protein, carbs and fat. May I suggest my Smoky Chipotle Hummus (page 135) with crackers or veggies? Or maybe my Lemon-Coconut Energy Balls (page 147) or Chocolate Oat Bars (page 139) for something sweet!

Whether you're running out the door or enjoying a slow weekend morning at home, I hope these easy vegan breakfast and snack recipes leave you feeling energized and satisfied during your day.

DECADENT RASPBERRY, ALMOND & CHOCOLATE CHIA PUDDING

Chia pudding is my secret weapon for a quick and easy breakfast or snack recipe. It takes less than 5 minutes to throw together, can be made in bigger batches for meal prep throughout the week and is a great source of plant-based omega-3s. If you struggle with getting enough plant-based protein at breakfast time, try making this with soy milk. It's best to make this recipe the night before you want to enjoy it, since it takes 4 to 6 hours to fully set. This chia pudding can be eaten on its own, or topped with other fruit, nuts or seeds, or any nut or seed butter of your choice!

1. Add the plant-based milk, chia seeds, cocoa powder, almond butter, maple syrup, vanilla extract and salt to a mason jar or a container with a lid. Whisk everything together until all of the ingredients are well combined, then refrigerate it for 10 minutes.

2. After 10 minutes, whisk all of the ingredients together again. You'll notice that the chia pudding has slightly thickened. Place it back in the fridge for at least 4 hours to let it thicken further. Note: This step is important to prevent clumps in your chia pudding.

3. Once you're ready to enjoy, top it with the raspberries. You can also add any additional toppings, like nut or seed butter, or other fruit, nuts or seeds.

4. Store leftovers in an airtight container in the fridge for up to 3 days.

RECIPE NOTES: Using soy milk in this recipe adds about 8 grams of protein per serving, which is why I prefer it.

Feel free to adjust the chia seed to plant-based milk ratio based on your preferences for thickness. This ratio of chia seeds to milk makes for a thick Greek yogurt–like consistency. If you prefer a thinner consistency, use just ¼ cup (40 g) of chia seeds, or adjust based on your preference. You can also mix in more milk after the chia pudding has set to thin it to your desired consistency.

If you don't typically like the texture of chia pudding, try blending all of the ingredients together, except the raspberries, before placing it in the fridge so you're left with a smooth pudding consistency.

GOOD SOURCE OF CALCIUM AND OMEGA-3

SERVES 2

PREP: 5 MINUTES
INACTIVE: 4 HOURS
TOTAL: ~4 HOURS

2 cups (480 ml) plant-based milk (I used soy milk)

¼ cup (40 g) + 2 tbsp (20 g) chia seeds

2 tbsp (15 g) cocoa powder

1 tbsp (15 g) almond butter

1 tbsp (15 ml) maple syrup

1 tsp vanilla extract

Pinch of salt

¼ cup (31 g) fresh raspberries, for topping

OPTIONAL TOPPINGS

Chopped dried cranberries + chopped pecans

Fresh or frozen blueberries + almond slivers

Peanut butter + sliced banana

SERVES 1-2

PREP: 5 MINUTES
TOTAL TIME: 5 MINUTES

2 pieces of bread

½ (19-oz [540-g]) can
chickpeas or white beans,
drained and rinsed

1 ripe avocado

2 tbsp (30 ml) lemon juice,
about ½ lemon

1 tsp nutritional yeast

½ tsp smoked paprika

⅛ tsp salt

⅛ tsp pepper

PROTEIN-PACKED AVOCADO TOAST

I like avocado toast as much as the next person, but if I'm eating something for breakfast, I want it to have a good source of protein, carbohydrates and fat. While avocado toast does have fat and carbohydrates, it's not a great source of protein. I've added chickpeas to this avocado toast recipe to boost the protein, fiber, iron and calcium! I also decided to add nutritional yeast and smoked paprika for a little extra flavor and flare!

1. Toast your bread.

2. Meanwhile, in a large bowl, mash together the chickpeas, avocado, lemon juice, nutritional yeast, smoked paprika, salt and pepper.

3. Spread the mixture on your toast and enjoy!

4. Refrigerate leftovers in an airtight container for up to 2 days.

RECIPE NOTE: Choosing whole grain bread provides more fiber and nutrients than white bread. To get even more nutrition in, try using a sprouted bread! Sprouting grains allows nutrients like iron, zinc and magnesium in the bread to be more easily absorbed by the body.

PEANUT BUTTER– CINNAMON LOW-SUGAR GRANOLA

GOOD SOURCE
OF IRON,
ONE-POT RECIPE,
30-MINUTE MEAL

There's something about the satisfying crunch of granola that just hits the spot. While I love the convenience of store-bought granolas, I don't love how much sugar they usually have. I'm totally fine eating added sugar from time to time, but I'd rather eat a cookie that I truly crave and enjoy than have it snuck into foods like granola and cereals. Because of that, I developed this low-sugar granola recipe that still tastes just as good as regular granola, without tons of sugar or oil. The result is a slightly sweet, nutty granola that pairs perfectly with plant-based milk or yogurt, or even on its own as a snack. It also stores well in an airtight container, so feel free to double or even triple the batch!

MAKES 4 CUPS OF
GRANOLA (440 G)

PREP: 10 MINUTES
COOK: 20 MINUTES
TOTAL: 30 MINUTES

1½ cups (120 g) large flake oats

½ cup (50 g) nuts, roughly chopped

1 tsp cinnamon

¼ tsp salt

¼ cup (60 g) natural peanut butter

2 tbsp (30 ml) coconut oil, melted

2 tbsp (30 ml) maple syrup

1 tsp vanilla extract

1. Preheat the oven to 350°F (176°C) and line a baking sheet with parchment paper.

2. In a large bowl, combine the oats, nuts, cinnamon and salt.

3. In a medium bowl, whisk together the peanut butter, coconut oil, maple syrup and vanilla extract. Pour the wet ingredients into the dry ingredients and mix well to combine.

4. Spread the granola on the baking sheet evenly and bake for 20 minutes, or until the granola begins to turn golden brown, stirring halfway through. Be careful not to burn the granola. Allow it to cool completely before serving, as it will crisp up as it cools.

5. Store leftovers in an airtight container for up to 2 weeks.

RECIPE NOTES: I used a mix of walnuts, cashews and hazelnuts for this recipe, but any nuts or seeds will work well.

SUN-DRIED TOMATO & BROCCOLI "EGG" BITES

MAKES 6 "EGG" BITES

PREP: 5 MINUTES
COOK: 20 MINUTES
TOTAL: 25 MINUTES

1 cup (92 g) chickpea flour

¼ cup (44 g) nutritional yeast

1 tsp garlic powder

1 tsp onion powder

1 tsp salt

½ tsp pepper

1 tbsp (15 ml) olive oil

1 tbsp (15 ml) oil from the sun-dried tomatoes

1 cup (240 ml) plant-based milk (I used unsweetened soy milk)

1 cup (91 g) broccoli florets, chopped

¼ cup (14 g) sun-dried tomatoes, diced

Egg bites have exploded in popularity over the past few years, likely because they're super convenient and packed with protein. Obviously, with the main ingredient being eggs, finding a plant-based alternative can be a bit challenging . . . until now. These Sun-dried Tomato & Broccoli "Egg" Bites use chickpea flour as the main ingredient, which is a great source of protein, fiber and iron and takes on the flavor of whatever it's seasoned with. It's also a great option if you want to include beans in your eating pattern but don't love the texture of them. I added sun-dried tomatoes and broccoli to this recipe to add some extra flavor and nutrients, plus nutritional yeast for a cheesy flavor. These are the perfect convenient, grab-and-go option for those busy days that the whole family will love!

1. Preheat the oven to 350°F (176°C) and grease a muffin tin, or line it with muffin liners.

2. In a large bowl, whisk together the chickpea flour, nutritional yeast, garlic powder, onion powder, salt and pepper.

3. Add the olive oil, oil from the sun-dried tomatoes and plant-based milk. Mix everything together well. Fold in the broccoli florets and sun-dried tomatoes.

4. Pour the chickpea batter into the muffin tin, adding about ⅓ cup (80 g) to each slot. Bake for 20 minutes, or until the chickpea batter is cooked through the center. Let them cool for 10 minutes before eating.

5. Refrigerate leftovers in an airtight container for up to 4 days, or store them in the freezer for up to 1 month. To warm or thaw after freezing, microwave them at 30-second intervals until thawed and warmed.

RECIPE NOTES: To make this recipe even easier, use frozen broccoli florets. You'll need to ensure they're chopped small enough before adding them to the batter, so I recommend thawing them in the microwave or by steaming so you can easily chop them.

Feel free to double this recipe and freeze leftovers to have as an easy grab-and-go breakfast or snack.

Use soy milk in this recipe for an extra boost of protein!

MY EVERYDAY ULTIMATE GREEN SMOOTHIE

SERVES 1

PREP: 5 MINUTES
TOTAL: 5 MINUTES

I'm a creature of habit, and one habit I've kept up for years is having a big smoothie for breakfast most mornings. I love how quick and easy smoothies are, and that they're a simple way to pack a lot of foods in that might be more challenging to incorporate at other times throughout the day, like seeds and greens. I often get asked how to make smoothies more filling, and my number one tip, as always, is to make sure that you're adding a good source of protein, carbohydrates and fat. It's also important to make sure that your smoothies are big enough to be considered a meal. If you want to have a smoothie for breakfast but also need to chew food to feel satisfied, try pairing it with a piece of Protein-Packed Avocado Toast (page 116) or a Sun-dried Tomato & Broccoli "Egg" Bite (page 120)! This smoothie may look super green, but I promise it's so tasty. If you're just getting used to adding greens to your smoothie, start with a small handful of spinach and work your way up.

1-3 cups (30–90 g) spinach or (67–201 g) kale, depending on your preference

1 ripe banana

1 cup (149 g) frozen strawberries or other berries of choice

2 tbsp (20 g) flax or chia seeds

1 tbsp (15 g) natural peanut butter

1 cup (240 ml) soy milk

½–1 cup (120–240 ml) water to blend, if needed

OPTIONAL ADD-IN

1 scoop plant-based protein powder

1. Add the spinach, banana, strawberries, flax seeds, peanut butter, soy milk and water to a high-speed blender and blend until smooth.

RECIPE NOTES: If you'd like to prep several servings of the ingredients for this smoothie ahead of time, add the smoothie's portioned spinach, banana and frozen strawberries to a freezer baggie. Do this for as many smoothies as you'd like to prep, so you have one smoothie serving in each baggie. When it comes time to make your smoothie, simply dump the contents of one baggie into the blender, add the flax or chia, peanut butter and soy milk and blend.

SERVES 1

PREP: 5 MINUTES
TOTAL: 5 MINUTES

1 ripe frozen banana (see
Recipe Notes)

1 cup (30 g) spinach

1 tbsp (15 g) natural peanut
butter

1 tbsp (7 g) cocoa powder

1 tbsp (10 g) chia seeds

1 cup (240 ml) soy or pea milk
(see Recipe Notes)

Pinch of salt

CHOCOLATE-PEANUT BUTTER SMOOTHIE

If you're looking for a quick, simple smoothie recipe that tastes like dessert, this Chocolate-Peanut Butter Smoothie is it. My trick for making satisfying smoothies is ensuring there's a good balance of protein, carbohydrates, fat and, of course, lots of delicious flavor! This smoothie uses soy milk for protein, a banana for carbohydrates, chia seeds and peanut butter for fat and cocoa powder to make it taste super chocolatey. I even added a handful of spinach for extra nutrients. If you're skeptical of adding spinach into a smoothie, I promise you won't even taste it!

1. Add the banana, spinach, peanut butter, cocoa powder, chia seeds, soy milk and salt to a high-speed blender and blend until smooth.

RECIPE NOTES: I like using a frozen banana in this smoothie since it makes it extra creamy, but feel free to use a fresh banana and add ice to the smoothie instead. The riper the banana is, the sweeter the smoothie will be!

I recommend using soy or pea milk in this recipe since they have 7 grams of protein per cup, whereas other plant-based milks typically only have 1 to 4 grams per cup.

SIMPLE CINNAMON BLENDER PANCAKES

On the weekends, it's tradition that my partner and I take our time making breakfast. It probably came from my dad, who loves making brunch for our family. His specialty is breakfast potatoes, which are the inspiration for my One-Pan Breakfast Hash (page 131), but sometimes I crave a sweet breakfast, which is where these Simple Cinnamon Blender Pancakes come in. I love that these pancakes are made in the blender, since it makes cleanup super easy. They're a little more nutrient dense and less fluffy than traditional pancakes, since we use oats to add some fiber and iron to the batter, but they're still super delicious. I recommend making a big batch of these on the weekend to freeze and heat in the toaster for a quick and easy weekday pancake breakfast!

1. Add the oats, flour, banana, maple syrup, plant-based milk, cinnamon, salt, baking powder and vanilla extract to a high-speed blender and blend until it's just smooth. Do not over blend; otherwise the pancakes won't rise as much.

2. Heat a large nonstick pan with 1 tablespoon (15 g) of vegan butter over medium heat. After a few minutes, flick a small amount of water onto the pan. If the water instantly sizzles, the pan is ready for the pancakes.

3. Pour the batter into the pan, with each pancake about 4 inches (10 cm) in diameter. Let them cook for 3 to 4 minutes on one side, or until you see the surface of the pancakes covered in bubbles. Flip the pancakes, and let them cook on the other side for an additional 3 to 4 minutes, being careful not to burn them.

4. Repeat step 3 until all the batter has been used, adding more vegan butter to the pan as necessary. Add any desired toppings.

5. Refrigerate leftovers in an airtight container for up to 3 days, or freeze leftovers for up to 3 weeks.

RECIPE NOTES: I recommend using soy milk in this recipe to add some protein to the pancakes!

It's important to use large flake oats in this recipe, as quick oats or steel cut oats won't result in the correct texture.

GOOD SOURCE OF FIBER, ONE-POT MEAL, 30-MINUTE MEAL

MAKES 8 MEDIUM-SIZED PANCAKES

PREP: 5 MINUTES
COOK: 20 MINUTES
TOTAL: 25 MINUTES

¾ cup (60 g) large flake oats

¾ cup (90 g) all-purpose flour

1 ripe banana

1 tbsp (15 ml) maple syrup or other sugar

1¼ cups (300 ml) plant-based milk (I used unsweetened soy milk, see Recipe Note)

1 tsp cinnamon

¼ tsp salt

1 tsp baking powder

1 tsp vanilla extract, optional

1–2 tbsp (15–30 g) vegan butter or coconut oil, for cooking the pancakes

OPTIONAL TOPPINGS

Maple syrup

Peanut butter

Berries or fruit

Vegan butter

SERVES 1

PREP: 5 MINUTES
INACTIVE: 6–8 HOURS
TOTAL: ~6–8 HOURS

1 carrot, grated (about ½ cup [72 g] once grated)

½ cup (40 g) large flake rolled oats

1 tbsp (10 g) chia seeds

1 tbsp (15 ml) maple syrup

1 tsp vanilla

1 tsp cinnamon

⅛ tsp nutmeg

Pinch of cloves

1 cup (240 ml) plant-based milk (I used unsweetened soy milk, see Recipe Notes)

OPTIONAL TOPPINGS

Plant-based yogurt

Walnuts

CARROT CAKE OVERNIGHT OATS

It's a well-known fact amongst family and friends that my mom makes the best carrot cake. It's the recipe that's requested at every celebration, and when I stopped eating eggs and dairy, she even veganized the recipe for me. It's such a nostalgic recipe for me that I find myself craving carrot cake flavors pretty often, which is why I came up with this Carrot Cake Overnight Oats recipe. It has the same sweet, cinnamon taste of carrot cake while being a more well-rounded option than eating a piece of cake for breakfast. Now, I'm definitely not saying these overnight oats are quite as delicious as carrot cake (because what could be?), but they make a good option when I want something a little more nutritious for breakfast. Overnight oats are a super simple breakfast option that can be made the night before, so all you have to do in the morning is heat them up, or eat them straight out of the jar!

1. Combine the carrots, oats, chia seeds, maple syrup, vanilla, cinnamon, nutmeg, cloves and plant-based milk in a container or mason jar and mix everything well. Let it sit in the fridge overnight, for 6 to 8 hours. Add optional toppings in the morning, if desired.

2. Refrigerate leftovers for up to 3 days.

RECIPE NOTES: I recommend using soy milk to add protein to this recipe.

If you're heating the overnight oats, scoop the oats into a bowl and microwave them for 1 minute.

If you're heating on the stove top, add an additional splash of plant-based milk, and heat them in a small pot over medium heat until heated through, 4 to 5 minutes.

ONE-PAN BREAKFAST HASH

In my family, we have a few staple recipes that bookmark special occasions. My mom's carrot cake for birthdays and celebrations, her mandarin orange salad and French onion soup on Christmas Eve and my dad's famous breakfast potatoes for Sunday brunches. My dad has been making these breakfast potatoes on the weekends for my family for as long as I can remember, so they're super nostalgic for me. While the rest of the family eats them with eggs, I wanted to create a breakfast hash that uses these potatoes with a good source of plant-based protein to round it out and make it a more satisfying breakfast. For this recipe, we combine a protein-packed tofu scramble with lots of veggies and my dad's famous breakfast potatoes to make a well-rounded breakfast hash that can be eaten on its own or in a wrap. Feel free to top it with salsa or vegan cheese! This makes for a super satisfying breakfast that's great for a chill weekend morning, and you can even save leftovers to eat throughout the week!

SERVES 4

PREP: 10 MINUTES
COOK: 40 MINUTES
TOTAL: 50 MINUTES

3 medium yellow potatoes, diced

1 tbsp (15 ml) + 1 tsp olive oil, divided

¾ tsp salt, divided, or to taste

½ tsp dried oregano

⅛ tsp chili flakes

1 yellow onion, diced

1 red bell pepper, diced

5 oz (142 g) cremini mushrooms, sliced

3 cloves garlic, minced

¼ tsp pepper

1 (12-oz [350-g]) block extra firm tofu, crumbled

1 tsp chili powder

½ tsp smoked paprika

3 tbsp (33 g) nutritional yeast

½ tsp garlic powder

2 tbsp (30 ml) plant-based milk (I used unsweetened oat milk)

1 cup (67 g) kale, chopped

1. Add the potatoes to a large pot and cover them with water. Bring the potatoes to a boil with the lid on. Immediately after the potatoes have come to a boil, remove them from the heat and drain off the water. Do not over boil the potatoes or else they will turn mushy when frying.

2. Add the potatoes to a large pan with 1 tablespoon (15 ml) of olive oil, ¼ teaspoon of salt, the oregano and chili flakes. Sauté everything with the lid on until the potatoes become almost fork tender, about 12 minutes. Stir the potatoes occasionally, but allow them to become golden brown on all sides.

3. Once the potatoes are almost fork tender, add the onion, 1 teaspoon of olive oil and ¼ teaspoon of salt to the pan, and sauté them until the onion is translucent and the potatoes are completely fork tender, about 3 to 4 minutes.

4. Add the bell pepper, mushrooms, garlic, ¼ teaspoon of salt and pepper. Sauté everything for an additional 5 minutes.

5. Add the tofu, chili powder, smoked paprika, nutritional yeast, garlic powder and plant-based milk. Sauté everything for an additional 5 minutes.

6. Add the kale and sauté until it's wilted.

7. Refrigerate leftovers in an airtight container for up to 4 days.

MAKES 2 CUPS (500 G)

PREP: 5 MINUTES
TOTAL TIME: 5 MINUTES

1 (19-oz [540-g]) can white
beans, drained and rinsed

2 tbsp (30 ml) olive oil

2 tbsp (30 ml)
balsamic vinegar

3 tbsp (45 g) tahini

1 tsp dried rosemary

1 clove garlic

½ tsp salt, or to taste

2 tbsp (30 ml) lemon juice,
about ½ lemon

WHITE BEAN, BALSAMIC & ROSEMARY DIP

I love having easy snack options in the fridge, and this White Bean, Balsamic & Rosemary Dip is one of my favorites. It's similar to hummus but has a creamier texture due to the white beans, and the balsamic rosemary flavor is perfect for pairing with crackers, veggies or even in a sandwich. It would also be perfect on a plant-based charcuterie board, since it's a bit more elevated than your usual bean dip. White beans are a great source of protein, fiber, iron and calcium, which are all important nutrients to focus on getting enough of. I recommend making this ahead of a busy week to snack on!

1. Add the white beans, olive oil, balsamic vinegar, tahini, rosemary, garlic, salt and lemon juice to a high-speed blender and blend until completely smooth.

2. Refrigerate leftovers in an airtight container for up to 5 days.

RECIPE NOTE: Try adding this White Bean, Balsamic & Rosemary Dip to a plant-based charcuterie board! I love pairing it with crackers, green olives, my favorite vegan cheese, nuts and fruit for a well-rounded board that guests will love!

SMOKY CHIPOTLE HUMMUS

GOOD SOURCE
OF IRON,
10-MINUTE MEAL

MAKES 2 CUPS (500 G)

PREP: 10 MINUTES
TOTAL: 10 MINUTES

As much as I appreciate the convenience of store-bought hummus, nothing beats homemade for me. I love how easily customizable homemade hummus is, and that we can control the amount of oil and salt that's added. Plus, it only takes 10 minutes to whip up and has just a few simple ingredients! This Smoky Chipotle Hummus is the perfect pairing for veggies or crackers, but it also tastes amazing spread onto a sandwich or scooped into a salad. The main ingredients are chickpeas, tahini and chipotle peppers in adobo sauce, which can be easily found at most grocery stores. This hummus definitely has a kick to it, but you can adjust the amount of chipotle peppers based on your spice preference. I recommend making a batch of this hummus for an easy and delicious snack to have throughout the week!

1 (19-oz [540-g]) can chickpeas, drained and rinsed

3 tbsp (45 g) tahini

¼ cup (60 ml) lemon juice, about 1 lemon

1–2 chipotle peppers in adobo sauce

3 tbsp (45 ml) olive oil

½ tsp salt, or to taste

2–3 tbsp (30–45 ml) additional oil or water, as needed

1. Add the chickpeas, tahini, lemon juice, chipotle peppers, olive oil and salt to a high-speed blender or food processor and blend until it's completely smooth. You may need to add additional oil or water 1 tablespoon (15 ml) at a time to reach your desired consistency.

2. Refrigerate leftovers in an airtight container for up to 5 days.

RECIPE NOTES: The trick for making extra creamy hummus is to make sure you blend it for long enough. I recommend 3 to 4 minutes, until it's completely smooth. To make it even creamier, you can remove the skins of the chickpeas by spreading them on a clean dish towel and rubbing them with another towel, but I usually skip this step.

If you don't love spicy hummus, try subbing the chipotle peppers with ¼ cup of sun-dried tomatoes, olives or pine nuts.

SUPER SIMPLE LENTIL BRUSCHETTA DIP

Even though I develop recipes as part of my job, whenever I get invited somewhere and want to bring a dish to share, I'm kind of at a loss for what to provide. Rather than bringing the classic chips and salsa, I've started bringing this Super Simple Lentil Bruschetta Dip instead! It requires just a few ingredients, but is packed with plant-based protein, fiber and iron from the lentils, plus super fresh flavor from the tomato bruschetta. Of course, this isn't authentic bruschetta, but it's inspired from the flavors and is absolutely delicious. I recommend serving this with a sliced, lightly toasted baguette or crunchy, seedy crackers. It's perfect for snacking or adding to the top of a salad for a flavorful punch!

SERVES 4

PREP: 15 MINUTES
TOTAL: 15 MINUTES

1 (19-oz [540-g]) can lentils, drained and rinsed

3 cups (450 g) cherry tomatoes, quartered (or 3 large Roma tomatoes, finely diced)

2 large cloves garlic, minced

2½ tbsp (38 ml) balsamic vinegar

3 tbsp (45 ml) olive oil

¼ cup (6 g) packed basil, julienned

¾ tsp salt, or to taste

FOR SERVING

Sliced, lightly toasted baguette or crackers

1. Add the lentils, tomatoes, garlic, balsamic vinegar, olive oil, basil and salt to a large bowl and stir it well to combine. Serve on slices of baguette or crackers.

2. This recipe is best enjoyed fresh, but can be refrigerated for up to 2 days in an airtight container.

RECIPE NOTE: Some of the juices from the tomatoes will settle to the bottom of the bowl. Feel free to drain this off, understanding that you may lose some of the flavor if you choose to do so.

CHOCOLATE OAT BARS

Growing up, I was the world's biggest chocolate lover. Chocolate bars, chocolate chip cookies, chocolate ice cream . . . anything chocolate, I wanted it. Nowadays I'm more of a savory person, but that doesn't mean I don't still get the craving for something sweet now and then. These Chocolate Oat Bars are perfect for those times since they're so simple to make, use ingredients you likely already have on hand and have less sugar than most snack and dessert bars. Oh, and did I mention they don't require any baking? Just combine the bar ingredients, press into a loaf tin, drizzle with chocolate and put in the freezer for 10 minutes! These make a delicious sweet snack or dessert and are totally kid-approved.

1. Line a loaf tin with parchment paper.

2. In a large bowl, stir together the oat flour, large flake oats and salt.

3. In a separate bowl, whisk together the coconut oil, maple syrup, peanut butter, plant-based milk and vanilla until well combined.

4. Pour the wet ingredients into the dry ingredients and stir them well to combine. It will be a thick dough.

5. Spoon the dough into the loaf tin. Using clean hands, press the oat mixture to the bottom of the tin until it's evenly distributed.

6. Pour the melted chocolate on top of the oat mixture, and use the back of a spoon to spread it evenly. Place in the freezer for at least 10 minutes or until it's set.

7. Refrigerate leftovers for up to 5 days.

RECIPE NOTES: To make your own oat flour, simply blend oats in a high-speed blender or food processor until they form a flour-like consistency.

I've used peanut butter in this recipe, but feel free to swap it for almond butter, sunflower seed butter or tahini.

GOOD SOURCE OF IRON, 30-MINUTE MEAL

SERVES 8

PREP: 15 MINUTES
INACTIVE: 10 MINUTES
TOTAL: 25 MINUTES

1 cup (88 g) oat flour (see Recipe Notes)

½ cup (40 g) large flake oats

½ tsp salt

2 tbsp (30 ml) coconut oil, melted

¼ cup (60 ml) maple syrup

½ cup (120 g) natural peanut butter (see Recipe Notes)

2 tbsp (30 ml) plant-based milk (I used unsweetened oat milk)

1 tsp vanilla

1 cup (170 g) chocolate chips, melted

SWEET & SPICY EDAMAME

SERVES 1

PREP: 2 MINUTES
COOK: 3 MINUTES
TOTAL: 5 MINUTES

1 cup (155 g) shelled edamame,
fresh or frozen
1 tsp maple syrup
1 tsp soy sauce
1 tsp sesame oil
¼ tsp chili flakes

If you follow me on social media, chances are you know I'm obsessed with edamame. I love that it's high in protein and iron and can be found in the freezer section of most grocery stores. Plus, it's super easy to add into meals and can even be eaten as a snack! If you've been to a Japanese restaurant, you've probably had edamame in the pod sprinkled with salt. This edamame recipe is sweet and spicy and takes less than 5 minutes to make! I used frozen, shelled edamame for this recipe, but if unshelled is all you can find, that will work too.

1. Place the edamame in a heat-safe bowl. Microwave the edamame in a splash of water for 2 to 3 minutes, or pour boiling water over top and let it sit for 2 to 3 minutes, until warmed through. Drain off the excess water.

2. Add the maple syrup, soy sauce, sesame oil and chili flakes to the edamame. Stir everything well to combine.

3. This recipe is best served fresh!

RECIPE NOTES: Edamame is a great quick and easy protein staple to have on hand, since half a cup provides 9 grams of protein! Try adding it into stir fries, salads or even pastas.

HERBY ROASTED CHICKPEAS

GOOD SOURCE
OF PROTEIN,
ONE-POT MEAL,
30-MINUTE MEAL

Roasted chickpeas are a perfect snack to me. Crunchy, savory and high in protein . . . what's not to love? If you struggle to make roasted chickpeas crispy, it's important to make sure that they're well spaced out on the baking sheet to ensure that they roast instead of steam. It's also important to make sure you're roasting at a high enough temperature, and for long enough. As roasted chickpeas cool, they'll get even crispier! Enjoy these as a snack, added to salads or as a topping on soup.

SERVES 4

PREP: 5 MINUTES
COOK: 20-25 MINUTES
TOTAL: 25-30 MINUTES

1. Preheat the oven to 450°F (232°C) and line a baking sheet with parchment paper.

2. In a large bowl, toss together the chickpeas, olive oil, oregano, garlic powder, dried rosemary and salt.

3. Spread the chickpeas evenly on the baking sheet, ensuring that there's enough room between the chickpeas. Roast for 20 to 25 minutes, until the chickpeas are golden brown. Let them cool.

4. Refrigerate leftovers in an airtight container for up to 5 days.

RECIPE NOTES: These chickpeas can also be made in an air fryer. I recommend setting the temperature to 400°F (204°C) and cooking them for 15 to 20 minutes, or until they're golden brown.

1 (19-oz [540-g]) can chickpeas, drained and rinsed

1 tbsp (15 ml) olive oil

1 tsp dried oregano

1 tsp garlic powder

1 tsp dried rosemary

¼ tsp salt

MAKES 10 DATES

PREP: 15 MINUTES
INACTIVE: 15 MINUTES
TOTAL: 30 MINUTES

10 Medjool dates

3 tbsp (45 g) plus 1 tsp natural peanut butter

⅔ cup (114 g) chocolate chips, melted

Sprinkle of flaky sea salt

PEANUT BUTTER-CHOCOLATE MEDJOOL DATES

If you're craving something sweet that tastes like a more nutritious version of a chocolate bar, these Peanut Butter–Chocolate Medjool Dates are it. My grandfather used to love eating dates dipped in sugar, so whenever I eat them I think of him. If you've never had dates before, they have a sweet, caramel-like flavor that pairs perfectly with peanut butter and chocolate. Plus, dates are a great source of fiber, which helps us to stay feeling full for longer, with blood sugar balance and bowel movements. I love that these only take 15 minutes of active prep time, so they're the perfect quick and easy dessert or snack when you're craving something sweet.

1. Remove the pits from the dates and cut them in half lengthwise to open. Spread about 1 teaspoon of peanut butter on 5 halves of the dates, then add the other date half to make a sandwich.

2. Dip the dates in the melted chocolate and place them on a plate lined with parchment paper. Sprinkle the chocolate-covered dates with flaky sea salt.

3. Place the dates in the freezer for 15 minutes, or until the chocolate has set.

4. Refrigerate any leftovers in an airtight container for up to 5 days.

RECIPE NOTES: Medjool dates work best for this recipe since they're softer than other types of dates.

Feel free to store these dates in the freezer in an airtight container for up to 1 month.

LEMON-COCONUT ENERGY BALLS

If you want a snack recipe that tastes like a vacation, these Lemon-Coconut Energy Balls are for you. They have a zesty, coconut flavor that's perfectly sweet while also being a great source of healthy fats, particularly omega-3s from the hemp seeds, and fiber from the oats. These are a great recipe to meal prep ahead of a busy week when you need quick grab-and-go snacks or dessert, plus they're totally kid-approved!

1. Add the sunflower seeds to a high-speed blender and blend until smooth. Add the oats and blend until they have the consistency of flour.

2. Add the sunflower seeds and oats to a large bowl with the coconut oil, ½ cup (48 g) of shredded coconut, the lemon zest, lemon juice, maple syrup, hemp seeds and salt. Stir to combine everything into a dough-like consistency.

3. Form the dough into balls of 2 to 3 tablespoons (40 to 60 g) per ball. You should have approximately 12 balls.

4. Add the remaining ⅓ cup (32 g) of shredded coconut to a bowl and roll the energy balls in the coconut. Place them on a clean plate and refrigerate them for 20 to 30 minutes until they're set.

5. Refrigerate leftovers in an airtight container for up to 1 week.

RECIPE NOTE: These energy balls can be frozen for up to 1 month. When you're ready to enjoy, simply place them in the fridge to thaw a few hours before eating.

GOOD SOURCE OF OMEGA-3 AND FIBER

MAKES 12 ENERGY BALLS

PREP: 10 MINUTES
INACTIVE: 20–30 MINUTES
TOTAL: 30–40 MINUTES

½ cup (67 g) raw, hulled, unsalted sunflower seeds

1 cup (80 g) large flake oats

2 tbsp (30 ml) coconut oil, melted

½ cup + ⅓ cup (80 g) shredded coconut, divided

1 tsp lemon zest

¼ cup (60 ml) lemon juice, about 1 lemon

3 tbsp (45 ml) maple syrup

¼ cup (20 g) hemp seeds

¼ tsp salt

MAKES 12 MUFFINS

PREP: 15 MINUTES
COOK: 20 MINUTES
TOTAL: 35 MINUTES

FOR THE MUFFINS

1⅔ cups (203 g) whole wheat flour

1 cup (80 g) large flake rolled oats

2 tsp (10 g) baking powder

1 tsp baking soda

½ tsp salt

2 very ripe bananas, mashed, about ¾ cup

1 tbsp (10 g) chia seeds

1 cup (240 ml) plant-based milk of choice (I used unsweetened oat milk)

¼ cup (50 g) brown sugar

2 tbsp (30 ml) coconut oil or vegan butter, melted

1 tsp vanilla

1 apple, diced (I used Macintosh)

½ cup (58 g) frozen cranberries

FOR THE TOPPING

1 tbsp (15 g) vegan margarine or butter

¼ cup (50 g) brown sugar

¼ cup (36 g) chopped almonds or walnuts

3 tbsp (15 g) large flake oats

½ tsp cinnamon

CRANBERRY-APPLE-WALNUT MUFFINS

These Cranberry-Apple-Walnut Muffins are slightly sweet, tart and nourishing with oats, apple and whole wheat flour. The key to making these muffins sweet with only ½ cup (100 g) of added sugar is making sure your bananas are super ripe, ideally using ones with brown spots. Try these muffins for a quick and easy breakfast option, or as a delicious afternoon snack!

1. Preheat the oven to 350°F (176°C). Add muffin liners to a muffin tin.

2. To begin making the muffins, in a large bowl, combine the whole wheat flour, oats, baking powder, baking soda and salt. Whisk them to combine.

3. In a medium bowl, combine the mashed banana, chia seeds, plant-based milk, brown sugar, melted coconut oil and vanilla. Stir until they're well combined.

4. Add the wet ingredients to the dry ingredients and mix together until just combined. Add the diced apple and cranberries and stir until combined, being careful not to over stir.

5. In a small bowl, whisk together the margarine, brown sugar, almonds, oats and cinnamon for the topping.

6. Spoon the muffin batter into the muffin tin, using about ⅓ cup (42 g) of batter per muffin. Top each muffin with 1 tablespoon (15 g) of the topping. Bake for 20 to 22 minutes, until they're golden brown around the edges, but be careful not to burn the topping.

7. Store them in an airtight container for up to 5 days.

RECIPE NOTE: If your bananas aren't quite ripe but you still want to make these muffins, you can bake the bananas whole at 300°F (150°C) for 30 minutes, until they turn black.

PLANT-BASED MEAL PLAN

When I first adopted a plant-based diet, I had a pretty good handle on the foods that I wanted to remove from my eating pattern, but I remember feeling overwhelmed and confused about what foods I should be *including*. Finding new recipes and meal planning throughout the week became a great way for me to get a handle on what to eat when my week was busier than I expected or when I wanted to be prepared by going to the grocery store early. I love meal planning because it can save time, money and energy, and make your life easier.

But let's get one thing straight. This meal plan is not a prescriptive weight-management plan. This is simply an accumulation of the recipes included in this cookbook arranged throughout the month in a way that I think goes well together and will help to ensure you're getting a wide variety of nutrients throughout the day.

Every single person's needs are different, and while this plan may work for some, it may not work for others. You'll notice that I also didn't add specific portion sizes to meals. While most of my recipes serve 2 to 4 people, please follow your own fullness and hunger cues when eating. I also encourage you to stray from this plan if you're craving different meals that aren't included.

There are a few things to note about this meal plan. You'll notice that we rely on leftovers for most lunches. If you are cooking for a family, I recommend doubling the dinner recipes based on serving size so that you have quick and easy lunches ready to eat. You'll also notice that I didn't provide specific time slots for snacks, since everyone's hunger and fullness levels are different!

Lastly, I provided a list of the easy components of meals that can be prepped ahead of time on the weekend to help meals come together more seamlessly throughout the week. This includes things like washing and chopping vegetables, prepping sauces and simply making sure you have the correct ingredients on hand so you don't need to run to the grocery store throughout the week.

WEEK 1

PREP AHEAD

- Grocery shop for all ingredients
- Make two batches of Carrot Cake Overnight Oats (page 128)
- Make two batches of Smoky Chipotle Hummus (page 135)
- Make one batch of Chocolate Oat Bars (page 139)
- Chop vegetables for the Spicy Black Bean Tortilla Soup (page 56) and Best Ever Taco Salad (page 84)
- Wash and chop vegetables like carrots, celery and cucumbers to eat with the Smoky Chipotle Hummus (page 135)

	MONDAY	TUESDAY	WEDNES-DAY	THURSDAY	FRIDAY	SATURDAY	SUNDAY
BREAK-FAST	Carrot Cake Overnight Oats	Protein-Packed Avocado Toast (page 116)	Carrot Cake Overnight Oats	My Everyday Ultimate Green Smoothie (page 123)	My Everyday Ultimate Green Smoothie	Simple Cinnamon Blender Pancakes (page 127)	One-Pan Breakfast Hash (page 131)
LUNCH	15-Minute Sun-dried Tomatoes & White Beans and Toast (page 35)	Leftover Spicy Black Bean Tortilla Soup	Leftover Miso Dijon Glazed Tempeh Bowl	Leftover One-Pan Mushroom Gnocchi	Leftover Best Ever Taco Salad	Leftover Creamy Tomato Basil Soup	Leftover Easy Broccoli & Bok Choy Noodles
DINNER	Spicy Black Bean Tortilla Soup	Miso-Dijon Glazed Tempeh Bowl (page 76)	One-Pan Mushroom Gnocchi (page 50)	Best Ever Taco Salad	Creamy Tomato Basil Soup (page 59)	Easy Broccoli & Bok Choy Noodles (page 45)	Herby Lentil "Meatballs" & Garlic Bread (page 42)
SNACKS	Smoky Chipotle Hummus crackers & veggies Chocolate Oat Bars	Smoky Chipotle Hummus crackers & veggies Chocolate Oat Bars	Smoky Chipotle Hummus crackers & veggies Chocolate Oat Bars	Smoky Chipotle Hummus crackers & veggies Chocolate Oat Bars	Smoky Chipotle Hummus crackers & veggies Chocolate Oat Bars	Smoky Chipotle Hummus crackers & veggies Chocolate Oat Bars	Smoky Chipotle Hummus crackers & veggies Chocolate Oat Bars

WEEK 2

PREP AHEAD

- Grocery shop for all ingredients
- Make one batch of Peanut Butter–Cinnamon Low-Sugar Granola (page 119)
- Make one batch of Decadent Raspberry, Almond & Chocolate Chia Pudding (page 115)
- Make two batches of Herby Roasted Chickpeas (page 143)
- Make one batch of the Lemon-Coconut Energy Balls (page 147)
- Chop vegetables for the Savory Brussels Sprouts & Tofu Bacon Bowl (page 83), Nourishing Curry Lentil Stew (page 55) and Miso-Ginger Tofu Stir-Fry (page 28)

	MONDAY	TUESDAY	WEDNES-DAY	THURSDAY	FRIDAY	SATURDAY	SUNDAY
BREAK-FAST	Leftover One-Pan Breakfast Hash from last week's plan	Leftover Simple Cinnamon Blender Pancakes	Peanut Butter–Cinnamon Low-Sugar Granola with plant-based yogurt	Decadent Raspberry, Almond & Chocolate Chia Pudding	Decadent Raspberry, Almond & Chocolate Chia Pudding	Peanut Butter–Cinnamon Low-Sugar Granola with plant-based yogurt	One-Pan Breakfast Hash (page 131)
LUNCH	Leftover Herby Lentil "Meatballs" & Garlic Bread from last week's plan	Leftover Savory Brussels Sprouts & Tofu Bacon Bowl	Leftover Nourishing Curry Lentil Stew	Leftover Miso-Ginger Tofu Stir-Fry	Leftover Lemon-Tahini White Bean Caesar Salad	Leftover Sun-dried Tomato & Brussels Sprouts Pasta	Leftover Easy Lemon-Pepper Tofu Bowl
DINNER	Savory Brussels Sprouts & Tofu Bacon Bowl	Nourishing Curry Lentil Stew	Miso-Ginger Tofu Stir-Fry	Lemon-Tahini White Bean Caesar Salad (page 80)	Sun-dried Tomato & Brussels Sprouts Pasta (page 31)	Easy Lemon-Pepper Tofu Bowl (page 92)	Beet & Quinoa Salad with Maple Vinaigrette (page 91) with Curry Sweet Potato Fries with Maple-Dijon Dipping Sauce (page 101)
SNACKS	Herby Roasted Chickpeas Lemon-Coconut Energy Balls	Herby Roasted Chickpeas Lemon-Coconut Energy Balls	Herby Roasted Chickpeas Lemon-Coconut Energy Balls	Herby Roasted Chickpeas Lemon-Coconut Energy Balls	Herby Roasted Chickpeas Lemon-Coconut Energy Balls	Herby Roasted Chickpeas Lemon-Coconut Energy Balls	Herby Roasted Chickpeas Lemon-Coconut Energy Balls

WEEK 3

PREP AHEAD

- Grocery shop for all ingredients
- Make one batch of Peanut Butter–Chocolate Medjool Dates (page 144)
- Make one batch of the Sun-dried Tomato & Broccoli "Egg" Bites (page 120)
- Chop vegetables for Warming Vegetable & Chickpea Curry (page 23) and Peanut-Miso Tofu Noodle Bowl (page 36)
- Make the dressing for the Lemon, Lentil & Quinoa Salad (page 88)

	MONDAY	TUESDAY	WEDNES- DAY	THURSDAY	FRIDAY	SATURDAY	SUNDAY
BREAK- FAST	Leftover One-Pan Breakfast Hash from last week's plan	Sun-dried Tomato Broccoli "Egg" Bites and toast	Sun-dried Tomato Broccoli "Egg" Bites and toast	Chocolate–Peanut Butter Smoothie (page 124)	Protein-Packed Avocado Toast (page 116)	Simple Cinnamon Blender Pancakes (page 127)	Leftover Simple Cinnamon Blender Pancakes
LUNCH	Leftover Beet & Quinoa Salad with Maple Vinaigrette with Curry Sweet Potato Fries with Maple-Dijon Dipping Sauce from last week's plan	Leftover Warming Vegetable & Chickpea Curry	Leftover Peanut-Miso Tofu Noodle Bowl	Apple-Dill Chickpea Mash (page 32)	Leftover Spicy Creamy Fusilli Pasta	Leftover Apple-Dill Chickpea Mash	Vegan Tempeh BLT Sandwich (page 40)
DINNER	Warming Vegetable Chickpea Curry	Peanut-Miso Tofu Noodle Bowl	Brothy Vegetable Dumpling Soup (page 64)	Spicy Creamy Fusilli Pasta (page 39)	Lemon, Lentil & Quinoa Salad and Basil Pesto Potatoes (page 110)	Leftover Lemon, Lentil & Quinoa Salad and Basil Pesto Potatoes	Smoky Black Bean Chili (page 49)
SNACKS	Sweet & Spicy Edamame (page 140) Peanut Butter–Chocolate Medjool Dates	Sweet & Spicy Edamame Peanut Butter–Chocolate Medjool Dates	Sweet & Spicy Edamame Peanut Butter–Chocolate Medjool Dates	Sweet & Spicy Edamame Peanut Butter–Chocolate Medjool Dates	Sweet & Spicy Edamame Peanut Butter–Chocolate Medjool Dates	Sweet & Spicy Edamame Peanut Butter–Chocolate Medjool Dates	Sweet & Spicy Edamame Peanut Butter–Chocolate Medjool Dates

WEEK 4

PREP AHEAD

- Grocery shop for all ingredients
- Make two batches of the White Bean, Balsamic & Rosemary Dip (page 132)
- Make one batch of the Cranberry-Apple-Walnut Muffins (page 148)
- Wash and chop veggies to eat with the White Bean, Balsamic & Rosemary Dip
- Make two batches of the Carrot Cake Overnight Oats (page 128)
- Make one batch of the Sun-dried Tomato & Broccoli "Egg" Bites (page 120)
- Make the barbecue chickpeas for the Barbecue Chickpea Wraps (page 46)
- Cut the Brussels sprouts for the Lemon-Dill Potato Sheet Pan Meal (page 27)

	MONDAY	TUESDAY	WEDNES-DAY	THURSDAY	FRIDAY	SATURDAY	SUNDAY
BREAK-FAST	Carrot Cake Overnight Oats	Sun-dried Tomato & Broccoli "Egg" Bites with Toast	Carrot Cake Overnight Oats	Sun-dried Tomato & Broccoli "Egg" Bites with Toast	Chocolate–Peanut Butter Smoothie (page 124)	One-Pan Breakfast Hash (page 131)	Leftover One-Pan Breakfast Hash
LUNCH	Leftover Vegan Tempeh BLT Sandwich from last week's plan	Barbecue Chickpea Wraps	Leftover Lemon-Dill Potato Sheet Pan Meal	Creamy Dill Pickle Salad (page 95) with Protein-Packed Avocado Toast (page 116)	Leftover Lemon Chickpea Orzo Soup	Leftover Miso-Ginger Tofu Stir-Fry	Leftover Hearty Vegan Sausage Stew
DINNER	Leftover Smoky Black Bean Chili from last week's plan	Lemon-Dill Potato Sheet Pan Meal	Leftover Barbecue Chickpea Wraps with Creamy Dill Pickle Salad	Lemon Chickpea Orzo Soup (page 71)	Miso-Ginger Tofu Stir-Fry (page 28)	Hearty Vegan Sausage Stew (page 60)	Basil Lentil Pasta Salad (page 75)
SNACKS	White Bean, Balsamic & Rosemary Dip with crackers & veggies Cranberry-Apple-Walnut Muffins	White Bean, Balsamic & Rosemary Dip with crackers & veggies Cranberry-Apple-Walnut Muffins	White Bean, Balsamic & Rosemary Dip with crackers & veggies Cranberry-Apple-Walnut Muffins	White Bean, Balsamic & Rosemary Dip with crackers & veggies Cranberry-Apple-Walnut Muffins	White Bean, Balsamic & Rosemary Dip with crackers & veggies Cranberry-Apple-Walnut Muffins	White Bean, Balsamic & Rosemary Dip with crackers & veggies Cranberry-Apple-Walnut Muffins	White Bean, Balsamic & Rosemary Dip with crackers & veggies Cranberry-Apple-Walnut Muffins

Aune, Dagfinn, NaNa Keum, Edward Giovannucci, Lars T. Fadnes, Paolo Boffetta, Darren C. Greenwood, Serena Tonstad, Lars J. Vatten, Elio Riboli, and Teresa Norat. "Whole grain consumption and risk of cardiovascular disease, cancer, and all cause and cause specific mortality: systematic review and dose-response meta-analysis of prospective studies." *BMJ* 353 (2016).

Ahmad, Iftekhar U., Jeffrey D. Forman, Fazlul H. Sarkar, Gilda G. Hillman, Elisabeth Heath, Ulka Vaishampayan, Michael L. Cher, Fundagul Andic, Peter J. Rossi, and Omer Kucuk. "Soy isoflavones in conjunction with radiation therapy in patients with prostate cancer." *Nutrition and Cancer* 62, no. 7 (2010): 996–1000.

Cardoso, Bárbara R., Graziela B. Silva Duarte, Bruna Z. Reis, and Silvia MF Cozzolino. "Brazil nuts: Nutritional composition, health benefits and safety aspects." *Food Research International* 100 (2017): 9–18.

Carlsson-Kanyama, Annika, and Alejandro D. González. "Potential contributions of food consumption patterns to climate change." *The American Journal of Clinical Nutrition* 89, no. 5 (2009): 1704S–1709S.

Chen, X., and J. J. B. Anderson. "Isoflavones and bone: animal and human evidence of efficacy." *Journal of Musculoskeletal and Neuronal Interactions* 2, no. 4 (2002): 352–359.

Craig, Winston J., and Ann Reed Mangels. "Position of the American Dietetic Association: vegetarian diets." *Journal of the American Dietetic Association* 109, no. 7 (2009): 1266.

Ginde, Adit A., Mark C. Liu, and Carlos A. Camargo. "Demographic differences and trends of vitamin D insufficiency in the US population, 1988-2004." *Archives of Internal Medicine* 169, no. 6 (2009): 626–632.

Goyal, Manu S., and Marcus E. Raichle. "Glucose requirements of the developing human brain." *Journal of Pediatric Gastroenterology and Nutrition* 66, no. Suppl 3 (2018): S46.

Hamilton-Reeves, Jill M., Gabriela Vazquez, Sue J. Duval, William R. Phipps, Mindy S. Kurzer, and Mark J. Messina. "Clinical studies show no effects of soy protein or isoflavones on reproductive hormones in men: results of a meta-analysis." *Fertility and Sterility* 94, no. 3 (2010): 997–1007.

Lane, Darius JR, and Des R. Richardson. "The active role of vitamin C in mammalian iron metabolism: much more than just enhanced iron absorption!" *Free Radical Biology and Medicine* 75 (2014): 69–83.

Lepretti, Marilena, Stefania Martucciello, Mario Alberto Burgos Aceves, Rosalba Putti, and Lillà Lionetti. "Omega-3 fatty acids and insulin resistance: focus on the regulation of mitochondria and endoplasmic reticulum stress." *Nutrients* 10, no. 3 (2018): 350.

Liu, Ann G., Nikki A. Ford, Frank B. Hu, Kathleen M. Zelman, Dariush Mozaffarian, and Penny M. Kris-Etherton. "A healthy approach to dietary fats: understanding the science and taking action to reduce consumer confusion." *Nutrition Journal* 16, no. 1 (2017): 1–15.

Mangels, Reed, Virginia Messina, and Mark Messina. *The Dietitian's Guide to Vegetarian Diets.* Jones & Bartlett Learning (2011).

Maret, Wolfgang, and Harold H. Sandstead. "Zinc requirements and the risks and benefits of zinc supplementation." *Journal of Trace Elements in Medicine and Biology* 20, no. 1 (2006): 3–18.

Marini, Herbert, Francesca Polito, Elena Bianca Adamo, Alessandra Bitto, Francesco Squadrito, and Salvatore Benvenga. "Update on genistein and thyroid: an overall message of safety." *Frontiers in Endocrinology* 3 (2012): 94.

McDougall, John. "Plant foods have a complete amino acid composition." *Circulation* 105, no. 25 (2002): e197–e197.

Menzel, Juliane, Klaus Abraham, Gabriele I. Stangl, Per Magne Ueland, Rima Obeid, Matthias B. Schulze, Isabelle Herter-Aeberli, Tanja Schwerdtle, and Cornelia Weikert. "Vegan Diet and Bone Health—Results from the Cross-Sectional RBVD Study." *Nutrients* 13, no. 2 (2021): 685.

Messina, Mark. "Insights gained from 20 years of soy research." *The Journal of Nutrition* 140, no. 12 (2010): 2289S–2295S.

Messina, Mark, Shaw Watanabe, and Kenneth DR Setchell. "Report on the 8th international symposium on the role of soy in health promotion and chronic disease prevention and treatment." *The Journal of Nutrition* 139, no. 4 (2009): 796S–802S.

Millward, D. Joe. "Amino acid scoring patterns for protein quality assessment." *British Journal of Nutrition* 108, no. S2 (2012): S31–S43.

Millward, D. Joe. "Identifying recommended dietary allowances for protein and amino acids: a critique of the 2007 WHO/FAO/UNU report." *British Journal of Nutrition* 108, no. S2 (2012): S3–S21.

O'Leary, Fiona, and Samir Samman. "Vitamin B12 in health and disease." *Nutrients* 2, no. 3 (2010): 299–316.

Oseni, Tawakalitu, Roshani Patel, Jennifer Pyle, and V. Craig Jordan. "Selective estrogen receptor modulators and phytoestrogens." *Planta medica* 74, no. 13 (2008): 1656–1665.

Quagliani, Diane, and Patricia Felt-Gunderson. "Closing America's fiber intake gap: communication strategies from a food and fiber summit." *American Journal of Lifestyle Medicine* 11, no. 1 (2017): 80–85.

Reynolds, Andrew, et al. "Carbohydrate quality and human health: a series of systematic reviews and meta-analyses." *The Lancet* 393.10170 (2019): 434–445.

Reynolds, Edward. "Vitamin B12, folic acid, and the nervous system." *The Lancet Neurology* 5, no. 11 (2006): 949–960.

Saunders, Angela V., et al. "Iron and vegetarian diets." *The Medical Journal of Australia* 199.4 (2013): S11–S16.

Schwalfenberg, Gerry K., S. J. Genuis, and Michelle N. Hiltz. "Addressing vitamin D deficiency in Canada: a public health innovation whose time has come." *Public Health* 124, no. 6 (2010): 350–359.

Springmann, Marco, Michael Clark, Daniel Mason-D'Croz, Keith Wiebe, Benjamin Leon Bodirsky, Luis Lassaletta, Wim De Vries et al. "Options for keeping the food system within environmental limits." *Nature* 562, no. 7728 (2018): 519–525.

Tilman, David, and Michael Clark. "Global diets link environmental sustainability and human health." *Nature* 515, no. 7528 (2014): 518–522.

Tome, Daniel. "Criteria and markers for protein quality assessment—a review." *British Journal of Nutrition* 108, no. S2 (2012): S222–S229.

van Die, M. Diana, Kerry M. Bone, Scott G. Williams, and Marie V. Pirotta. "Soy and soy isoflavones in prostate cancer: a systematic review and meta-analysis of randomized controlled trials." *BJU International* 113, no. 5b (2014): E119–E130.

Watanabe, Fumio, and Tomohiro Bito. "Vitamin B12 sources and microbial interaction." *Experimental Biology and Medicine* 243, no. 2 (2018): 148–158.

World Health Organization/Food and Agriculture Organization/United Nations University. Expert Consultation. "Protein and amino acid requirements in human nutrition." *WHO Technical Report Series*, no. 935 (World Health Organization/Food and Agriculture Organization) 2007.

Yan, Lin, and Edward L. Spitznagel. "Soy consumption and prostate cancer risk in men: a revisit of a meta-analysis." *The American Journal of Clinical Nutrition* 89, no. 4 (2009): 1155–1163.

Zimmermann, Michael B. "Iodine deficiency." *Endocrine Reviews* 30, no. 4 (2009): 376–408.

ACKNOWLEDGMENTS

To Dean, my dad, for knowing absolutely everything about anything, for always being my first phone call and for never doubting that I could do this. I'm beyond lucky to have you. I love you bunches.

To Donna, my mom, for your unwavering support, for loving everything I make (unless it's tofu) and for always being proud of me, no matter what. I'm so lucky to be your daughter. I love you to the moon and back.

To Avery, for being my forever recipe tester, for constantly being there for me whether I need someone to laugh or cry with and for running to the grocery store when I inevitably forget an ingredient. You make life so much better.

To Andrew, for making my recipes, showing me cooking YouTube videos growing up even when I protested and for giving me someone to look up to. I'm so proud to be your little sister.

To Jeff, for inspiring me to go vegetarian, for being the best person to talk about new vegan foods with and for giving me someone to look up to. I'm so proud to be your little sister.

To my audience, for showing interest in this cookbook long before it was ever written and for allowing me to call this work. You inspire me every day.

To my friends, for telling everyone you know about T2T and for always making me feel like what I do is important. I'm beyond grateful for you all.

To Sarah and the team at Page Street Publishing, for bringing me on this journey and believing in me the whole way. I'm endlessly grateful.

ABOUT THE AUTHOR

Lauren McNeill is a plant-based registered dietitian and nutrition expert from Halifax, Nova Scotia, currently residing in Toronto. She runs the popular social media page @tastingtothrive_rd and her blog www.tastingtothrive.com where she shares plant-based recipes, nutrition and wellness information and debunks common plant-based myths. She holds a master's of public health in nutrition and dietetics with a collaborative specialization in women's health. Lauren is committed to bringing evidence-based information about plant-based nutrition to the masses and educating others on common misconceptions about eating. She values making plant-based eating approachable and inclusive, and truly believes that what we do eat is so much more important than what we don't eat.

Lauren has her own virtual nutrition private practice and online program where she counsels clients wherever they are on their plant-based journey, whether they've been vegan for years or simply want to incorporate more plant-based foods into their everyday eating pattern. She has developed plant-based nutrition and cooking programs for *Vegetarian Times*, has spoken at prestigious conferences such as the first-ever Plant-Based Nutrition Conference in Canada and has been frequently interviewed for news outlets such as Global News and the *Toronto Star*.

Follow Lauren on social media @tastingtothrive_rd and her blog www.tastingtothrive.com.

INDEX